# Elegy for Literature

# Elegy for Literature

Jeffrey T. Nealon

ANTHEM PRESS

Anthem Press
An imprint of Wimbledon Publishing Company
*www.anthempress.com*

This edition first published in UK and USA 2022
by ANTHEM PRESS
75–76 Blackfriars Road, London SE1 8HA, UK
or PO Box 9779, London SW19 7ZG, UK
and
244 Madison Ave #116, New York, NY 10016, USA

*British Library Cataloguing-in-Publication Data*
A catalogue record for this book is available from the British Library.

Library of Congress Control Number: 2021953407

ISBN-13: 978-1-83998-395-5 (Pbk)
ISBN-10: 1-83998-395-7 (Pbk)

This title is also available as an ebook.

# CONTENTS

# Chapter 1

# ENDGAMES

Finished, it's finished, nearly finished, it must be nearly finished.
—Samuel Beckett, *Endgame*

It will have given me no real joy to pen something with the grim title *Elegy for Literature*, especially under the specific circumstances of its composition. The graduate course that constituted the dry run for this book began in the opening weeks of 2020, and there we started out by looking at the various dire employment outlooks for graduate students in literary studies, and even more specifically in English—which is to say, elegies for the academic study of literature. We began by reading a newly released *Chronicle of Higher Education* collection of essays, ominously titled *Endgame: Can Literary Studies Survive?*[1] You don't have to be a particularly close or critical reader to guess the answer to the subtitling query, when the title already gives it away; but just in case there was any lingering ambiguity, the opening sentences clear things up: "The academic study of literature is no longer on the verge of field collapse. It's in the midst of it" (3); and this *Chronicle* special report promises to "offer a comprehensive picture of an unfolding catastrophe" (3). This, mind you, was *January* 2020—and that summation was describing essays that were largely written in 2018–19. By the time I typed these sentences in the Fall of 2020, any sense of a largely metaphorical meaning for "unfolding catastrophe" had faded into a literal pandemic nightmare called Covid-19. We closed out the second half of that graduate seminar over Zoom, students having been banished from campuses nationwide. It remains unclear what academia will look like going forward from the corona crisis, or whether workers from whole sectors of the global economy (bars, restaurants, retail stores, various travel, transportation and hospitality industries, and of course higher education) can recover from a year of virtual delivery or outright closure, as well as likely recurring waves of Covid-19 variants. And what to say about the well more than five million people globally, including over eight hundred thousand in the United States alone (as of mid-December, 2021) who will have lost their lives? Words fail.

Spring and Summer of 2020 also saw the beginnings of a long overdue and widespread national reckoning with the ongoing legacy of white supremacy in the United States, prompted by the horrific murder of George Floyd by police in Minneapolis. The Black Lives Matter movement has, among many other interventions, thrown a harsh reflective light on the academy and its role in furthering, however unwittingly or unconsciously, the American project of systematic white supremacy. The English department's literary canon, from "Beowulf to Virginia Woolf" as they say, will have some difficult explaining to do going forward into an anti-racist future, insofar as (until quite recently, given its thousand-year scope) most everyone included in that literary canon will have been a straightforward, unapologetic white supremacist—whether we like it or care to admit it, or not. I suppose it's easy enough to see why colonialist and orientalist fantasies like those harbored in Rudyard Kipling's work need to be shown the racist door; but even Walt Whitman, poster boy for all that is supposedly inclusive in nineteenth-century American literature, was a scurrilous white supremacist, to the point of prophesizing that the "inferior" races in North America—specifically, Africans and Native Americans—would, and indeed should, die out to make way for the inevitable triumph of what he called in another context the "superber race."[2] Endgame, indeed.

In short, it's very difficult these days to avoid the conclusion that the English department has been a junior partner in the project of white supremacy (just think of the way that "Shakespeare" functions as an unproblematic signifier for supposedly timeless, world-historical literary genius). And you don't need to look to fringe outside agitators to paint this damning picture of literary studies: as the web page of the University of Chicago's English Department puts it in a July 2020 "Faculty Statement," "English as a discipline has a long history of providing aesthetic rationalizations for colonization, exploitation, extraction, and anti-Blackness. Our discipline is responsible for developing hierarchies of cultural production that have contributed directly to social and systemic determinations of whose lives matter and why." (This characterization comes directly after the Department proudly touts itself as "ranked first among English Departments in the US," which seems to suggest that they're tops in "colonization, exploitation, extraction and anti-Blackness"?)[3]

Closer to home, my own English department has promised collective soul-searching concerning "our discipline's role in reproducing the racist history, legacy, and function of the university," as we look to put together an internal committee with the charge to "look critically at our curriculum and pedagogy to identify opportunities to combat racism and inequality." Which should probably entail cancelling 90 percent of said curriculum—if not the entire English department. Indeed, more than a half century ago postcolonial theorists like Ngugi wa Thiong'o were already calling for "The Abolition of the English

Department."[4] And I'm not sure that the recent push to rename the "English Department" as the "Department of Literatures in English" is really up to the task, and frankly seems a bit like swapping out the film title "Birth of a Nation" for the more accurate original name, "The Clansman": it seems as if we don't necessarily need to reshoot the white supremacist script that is the history of literature, nor refuse to distribute or publicize it. But let's at least give it a more saleable moniker, shall we? If such a call to walk away from the vast majority of English Literature (even under the newly baptized and undoubtedly more progressive guise of "Literatures in English") still seems too radical, I'd at least suggest that medievalists nationwide had best heed Chaucer's advice and be "slepen al the nyght with open ye."[5] In any case, these disparate factors, taken together, make historical English literature as a field of study seem like it has, to quote the great English poet John Lydon, "no future."[6]

While it remains unclear just how much the Covid-19 pandemic and the racial reckoning called for by the Black Lives Matter movement will intensify the demise or radical reorganization of academic literary study (or how those seismic events will influence the fate of anything else in the traditional humanities, for that matter), the upheavals of 2020 almost certainly will have accelerated what was an already dire state of affairs in terms of tenure-line hiring, recruiting majors, and maintaining institutional visibility for literary studies. As the essays in *Endgame* make clear, US literature departments never really recovered (in terms of hiring new tenure-line faculty members, or attracting new undergraduate students) from the 2008 economic downturn. As the familiar tale goes, that banking calamity led to most states further slashing their already diminished funding of higher education, thereby freezing tenure-line faculty hiring. And academic administrators, never ones to waste a crisis, turned instead to hiring armies of low-paid adjuncts with limited job security and zero academic freedom.

On the students' side, government funding cuts led to a boosting of already sky-high tuition rates, forcing students in turn to rethink the rising costs of a college degree in terms of return on their career investment. When times are tight, or so the narrative continues, the humanities and the arts begin to look like luxuries in the jaundiced eyes of deans and provosts, but they also look like bad investments to the customers (as we now refer to students). Likewise, if you're an academic administrator hoping to diversify your faculty or your core curriculum in the face of Black Lives Matter protests, the historical study of English literature seems like one of the last places you'd look to further that cause—especially after the discipline has so loudly and publicly denounced itself for furthering white supremacy. In short, for your dean, approving a job search for a new English department Miltonist is not going to be job one for quite a while, if ever.

When it came specifically to taxpayer funding for higher education after the 2008 crash in the United States, investing government money in the arts and humanities became a punching-bag talking point for politicians from both sides of the aisle—from the Democratic side, President Obama (BA economics) famously dissed art history as a major.[7] As far as English is concerned, it didn't help that 2012 Republican presidential nominee Mitt Romney (BA English) politely but decisively shat upon his former course of study: "As an English major I can say this: as an English major your options are, you better go to graduate school, alright? And find a job from there."[8] One might paraphrase, "as an English major, your options are that you have no options," especially when the primary thing it supposedly prepares you for—graduate study—has never been less attractive. Even the alternative careers that many of my colleagues have been touting for several years (students with advanced degrees can work for a museum or other cultural institution or an educational foundation) are looking like they're equally going to be taken by the grim reaper of Covid-19, at least in the short run (from which the long run may never recover—once museums, e.g., were closed or seriously curtailed for an extended period, bringing on inevitable layoffs, there proved to be a massive backlog of hungry museum workers long after cultural institutions haltingly reopened in mid-2021).

Likewise, as some colleges begin to cut faculty and potentially even close through the 2020s, they will release a large influx of experienced humanities teachers into an already saturated marketplace, making an already difficult academic job search nearly impossible to navigate not only for those seeking faculty positions, but also for folks searching for alt-ac careers more generally. If you think there's an oversupply of literature PhDs now, just wait a few years: after a combination of hiring freezes, the continued erosion of tenure-line hiring, and many new entrants thrown onto the market by college closings and departmental downsizings, the situation of 2019 (already diagnosed as bleak by the *Chronicle*) may in retrospect look like a golden era. Whatever lies on the road ahead, it seems uncontroversial to say that humanities departments like English never recovered (on either the student or faculty end) from the 2008 crash, and things are poised to get even worse in the wake of the early 2020s and their seismic ruptures to the cultural and socioeconomic landscape.

## Literature—What's It Good For?

To make a slight return to the Chronicle's *Endgame* volume, there's plentiful disagreement among those fourteen essays concerning the severity of the present situation and whether there's a way forward for literary study; but there is one strange, subterranean connection that holds all of the essays together: with the exception of Simon During's essay on the history of literature as a category, all of these diagnoses of the present remain, however silently, premised on the idea of literature's enduring value, a sense of the literary that seems, for all but During, scarcely even to have a history. Many of these essays read, at least in subtext, like a parody of the Freshman Composition paper: "Since the beginning of time, literature has always been important on campus. This is even more true in today's modern world today." The problems plaguing the present and the future of academic literary study, such as they are diagnosed and discussed by most of these English professors, are uniformly characterized as exterior in origin—an anti-intellectual agenda prosecuted by corporate shills, STEM-shamers, ideological state legislators, neoliberal spin doctors, penny-pinching administrators, ballooning university endeavors not related to the academic mission, and so on. The picture you get in almost all these diagnoses is that literature, still the champ in the hearts and minds of students and the public, has been systematically stoned to death by a thousand small rocks, not unlike St. Stephen, the first Christian martyr.

The status of literature itself—what's it good for in the present?—comes up only somewhat orthogonally in the most contentious disagreement within the *Endgame* collection, between Michael Clune's position in "The Humanities' Fear of Judgment" and a critique of his argument penned by G. Gabrielle Starr and Kevin Dettmar ("Who Decides What's Good and Bad in the Humanities?"). Clune calls for English departments to reinvigorate aesthetic judgments about literary merit and value, against what he calls the "dogmatic equality" (40) of neoliberal marketplace opinion—beginning and ending with students saying "I like this book" or "I don't like this book." Clune sees this consumerist model, where the literary work is judged like any other commodity, as having overtaken the college literature classroom, the perhaps inevitable hangover from a feel-good K–12 English curriculum adapted from the Lake Wobegon model where everyone (and every aesthetic opinion) is above average. In response to Clune, Starr and Dettmar argue that an old-fashioned, top-down notion of literary value or merit can't be the driver of literary studies. Sure, they argue, value is a key component of an English curriculum, but not the sense of value as an Arnoldian aesthetic judgment concerning the best that's been thought and written. As Starr and Dettmar write, "Sit in on any English class and you'll hear a lot about value— about the value of pushing the boundaries of empathy; about the efficacy of poetry in encouraging thorough, expansive engagement, rather than minimal, uniform assessment; about the moral weight of fiction in a world that may be post-truth" (42).

Against Clune's call to return to stressing disciplinary imperatives (wherein students need to read and evaluate works according to agreed-upon criteria in order to gain "access to a domain of aesthetic, scientific, or literary value"), Starr and Dettmar argue for a mode of inquiry no longer based on the disciplinary aesthetics of norms, names, and movements—against the sense that you need to read Milton to understand Blake's Romanticism, for example— but based on what they call the "pleasure" of reading that develops "aesthetic empathy" (44): "We can show new pleasures and new ways of valuing things—we can embody them—but we can't make you feel them. We model a style of engagement, of critical thought: we don't transmit value" (44). Clune in turn rebukes Starr and Dettmar as dupes for neoliberalism, accusing them of using their classroom lecterns to shill for a shallow, corporate retreat version of "the values of difference and empathy" (46); in addition, Clune snarkily asks, "What exactly qualifies a literature PhD as an empathy expert? Why should students [...] go into debt to learn how to be moral from the authors of scholarly books on 18th-century literature and Bob Dylan?" (46). That initially seems like a good question: why become an English major if it's merely about branding yourself as a biopolitical subject whose primary expertise is virtue signaling? Clune even wonders, no doubt rhetorically, whether this new empathy curriculum is the reason why "English majors are at historic lows" (46)?

But Clune's dismissal of the biopolitical pedagogy of empathy and pleasure begs a prior question that seems even harder to answer in the present. Even if we leave aside for the moment biopolitical imperatives like individual consciousness raising, empathy, or pleasure, and follow Clune by directing our attention back to disciplinary questions about literary merit and interpretive judgment, this would seem to raise an even more troubling question: why should anyone become an English major if it's all about being able to diagnose why Shakespeare's *Hamlet* (first performed around 1600) is aesthetically superior to the English Renaissance revenge tragedies that came before it (Thomas Kyd's ca.1587 *The Spanish Tragedy* is said to have pioneered the genre) or after it (say, John Ford's incestuous blood fest *'Tis Pity She's a Whore*, published in 1633)? Why should Clune's distinctly disciplinary sense of aesthetic judgment unproblematically be recognized as knowledge, and a "valuable" college curriculum at that, while a student's biopolitical knowledge (of oneself, one's likes and dislikes, mixed with empathy for the likes and dislikes of others) seems not to qualify as knowledge at all (at least for Clune)? Undoubtedly, the wide range of reference to revenge tragedy in later canonical literary works (from T. S. Eliot's "The Waste Land" to Thomas Pynchon's *The Crying of Lot 49*) doesn't make much sense if you haven't taken the non-Shakespearean Renaissance drama course; but such disciplinary expertise seems like an awfully long way to go for a pretty weak payout (just so you get some textual sub-references later)?

Whatever its merits or values, much disciplinary knowledge remains herme(neu)tically sealed—referring largely to itself. In my own subfield of theory, for example, I will admit with alacrity that you'll never understand linguistic-turn structuralism or post-structuralism if you don't read Saussure on the arbitrary, synchronic nature of the connection between the signifier and the signified. But why would a student today want or need to understand structuralist or post-structuralist theory in the first place? That's a harder question to answer. And Clune's implied "you need to know it because that's how disciplines work" seems, much more so than asking students to read for empathy and pleasure, to be the reason why there are so few eager English majors among Generation Z, for whom such disciplinary "expertise" is a highly suspicious category. (Likewise, if empathy toward other points of view and biopolitical self-knowledge constitute such losers among the students today, it's very hard indeed to explain why creative writing constitutes the only growth sector left in the English portfolio.)

Before too hastily dismissing Clune as a run-of-the-mill conservative elitist, however, we would do well to remember that Clune is here further advancing his mentor Walter Benn Michaels's neo-Marxist case against the influence of biopolitical capitalism in education—trying to expose the student "choice and empowerment" model as a cruel bait and switch, where you're offered a supposed range of choices that in practice forces you each and every time to become a late-capitalist consumer, and thereby to affirm the individualizing dictates of neoliberal capitalism.[9] "Empathy" on this reading reduces concerns about structural inequality to the level of individual choices and consciousness enhancement, thereby taking everyone's eye off the systematic nature of oppression in American society. Think of the parallel neoliberal sense that health care, for example, finally comes down to my or your individual choices, or that wealth is supposedly equitably doled out to the most industrious individuals. Such consistent attempts to explain a systematic problem—unequal wealth distribution or access to health care—by reference individual beliefs and actions is characteristic of the neoliberal ideology across the board. Blame the victim—if you get sick and/or if you're poor, you must have made some bad decisions! And in the end, neoliberal capitalism's agenda of false choice and privatized individualism is Clune's primary target in his critiquing the pedagogy of pleasure and/or empathy. (To speak cryptically, the critique is more Theodor Adorno than it is Matthew Arnold—though of course, siding with Adorno hardly buys you out from under the charge of elitism.)

In any case, we could continue going round and round on this question—whether whatever future English has left will mirror its disciplinary past, dedicated to aesthetic judgments and the question of artistic merit; or whether literary study has morphed into a kind of alterity-training curriculum, learning to see the world through multiple others' eyes. But, however you want to slice it, these do seem to me the two justifications for our work that I hear mostly consistently offered up at English department meetings: (1) we're engaged in a primarily disciplinary exercise, introducing students to English and American literature and the methods by which they've been studied throughout the discipline's history; or (2) we're engaged in a largely biopolitical exercise, introducing students (through literature) to the ethical life of citizenship and compassion, primarily utilizing those methods of reading that will enrich the individual's respect for, and understanding of, the public sphere going forward.

There are surely other ways of understanding or thematizing the work of an English department, but I do believe these are the primary two in the present; and I will say right off the bat that, regardless of where you fall on that discipline versus biopower spectrum, and even if we all inevitably mix them up to some degree in everyday pedagogy (you begin the class discussion with students' subjective impressions before diving into the formal complexities of the work), in the long run there's no choosing: given the triumph of a biopolitical regime globally, the disciplinary understanding of knowledge ("You need to read Beaumont and Fletcher to see why Shakespeare really is great! And such knowledge will somehow help you escape the clutches of neoliberalism!") is as dead as the Pony Express going forward; and that notion of disciplinary expertise is water under the bridge in spaces that go far beyond the university, and for reasons that go far beyond any given college student's decision concerning a major. There's been a structural transformation of the public sphere in the internet era, which is also the age of the triumphant global neoliberal capitalism (after 1990). The style of empathetic virtue signaling (or its converse, "calling out") that Clune delights in skewering has, for better or worse, become the dominant form of everyday subjectivity in the social media era and will be the only possible throughline for a major like English or any other humanities enterprise—which is to say, majors that are invested in affective response as their primary pedagogical form and content.

You can, as Clune or Benn Michaels do, dismiss this form of empathy training as corporate neoliberal twaddle all you like, but it's what Black Lives Matter demands from the university as well. Look at what's being called out and called for: against the near-monotone whiteness of the present American university, activists are calling for more Black faculty and administrators, more training for everyone to recognize and value Black points of view, and a more representatively diverse curriculum. Given that link to the Black Lives Matter protests, it's pretty expensive (bordering on suicidal) to argue that activist students demanding such hiring and curriculum reforms and calling for additional modes of diversity training are simply dupes for neoliberalism—though that's exactly the route that Benn Michaels has taken, suggesting that anti-racism is simply the left flank of mainstream neoliberal ideology (which, by putting emphasis on individual or group identity, downplays broad-based class solidarity and wealth redistribution).[10]

Not to mention the fact that, in Clune's case, arguing explicitly for a "return to judgment" (a renewed appeal to those disciplinary "standards" that now function for many activists as a shorthand for white supremacy) hardly seems set to become the mechanism that saves the discipline of literary study, much less offering any chance to diversify it: the question, "is this a good short story?" has long been synonymous with "is the form and content of this short story in accordance with universalizing literary standards originally set in the 1930s and 40s by white males working at elite universities?" In his essay "Judgment and Equality," Clune insists that adherence to these very disciplinary standards will paradoxically set you free (from neoliberalism) by modeling what he calls "better, freer forms of human life": "The discipline of aesthetic education—with its norms, traditions, and modes of practice—represents, like every discipline [!], a relatively autonomous method for producing judgments. Dogmatic equality condemns this autonomy. The capitalist passion for equality conceals a hollowness at its core."[11] The fact that capitalism's appeals to equality are bogus is, I guess, a point well taken—though I'm not sure why you'd want or need to appeal to disciplinary standards of academic practice in literary studies to uncover this truism, when Thomas Piketty's work in economics bears it out in quite exhaustive detail.[12]

In addition, though Clune doesn't bring this up, if you want to attain this brand of lofty uncommodifiable aesthetic judgment, in the form of a BA degree in English, it will cost you around $280,000 at his home institution, Case Western Reserve University. Which seems at some odds with the claim that such disciplinary knowledge is "inassimilable to market exchange."[13] Even if you accept Clune's argument lauding the autonomy of aesthetic judgment, it's not at all clear that literature is the primary or privileged artform upon which such judgment should be exercised. Indeed if "every discipline" produces its own "relatively autonomous method for producing judgments," why should anyone major in English, or in the humanities more generally? Spending the weekend memorizing the periodic table of elements or doing algebra word problems seems, in the short term at least, just as "inassimilable to market exchange" as memorizing the opening lines of *The Canterbury Tales* or brushing up on the formal differences among various forms of sonnets.

Clune's appeal to aesthetic judgment, against the false dogmatic equality of the market, falls firmly (as well as flat) under the category "things highly-educated white guys like" (alongside other things one can find on Clune's CV, including a passion for video games, memoirs, degrees from Oberlin and Johns Hopkins, and Guggenheim awards). And at the end of the day, one of the things that such white guys like best is insisting on class critique as the only vanguard, effective politics—while denigrating identity concerns as a mere neoliberal distraction, all the while largely ignoring the real concerns of the people in that working class, who have very compelling reasons to shop at unaesthetic places like Walmart and rightly remain skeptical of the idea that being an English major can set you free. And while a sweeping dismissal of the "neoliberal" emphasis on identity is certainly a defensible argumentative position, I can't imagine how you argue that persuasively to the families of George Floyd, Breonna Taylor, Daniel Prude, Philando Castille, Eric Garner, Sandra Bland, Freddie Grey, Tamir Rice, Michael Brown, Osaze Osagie, and tragically far too many others to be able to say their names here.

## Theory—What's It Good For?

In my own corner of the literary studies field, "theory," the undergraduate curriculum has for a long time been quite insular in understanding its mission within a rigidly disciplinary paradigm. For much of my teaching lifetime, which is to say for the past thirty years, the North American contemporary theory survey course has been taught to undergraduates and graduate students on the model of a restaurant menu: let's see, I'll start with some formalism, both Russian and new critical, as an amuse-bouche, then move on to Saussure as the fast track to understanding structuralism (dutifully noting that it was dead on arrival at Hopkins in 1966, slain by latecomer to the program Jacques Derrida and his "Structure, Sign and Play" essay), then on to post-structuralism, new historicism, feminism, psychoanalysis, ethnic and race studies, queer theory, deconstruction, postcolonial studies, cultural Marxism, and so on until the fifteen-week traveling roadshow of a semester is exhausted—ending not with a bang, but the collective whimper solicited when all these "hermeneutics of suspicion" paradigms are undercut by newcomers like post-critical, distant, reparative, and/or descriptive reading.

Such an approach has for just as long been understood as problematic—among many other critiques of this model, one might lament the lockstep historicism, the implied progress narratives, the synecdochic problem of one or two theorists standing in for whole movements, and so on. But here I would highlight the fact that the survey course too often asks students merely to apply paradigms uncritically to literary and other cultural texts—suggesting that theory is thoroughly instrumental and disciplinary in nature. In short, the menu model strongly suggests that the theories themselves are interchangeable templates to be put to use in a disciplinary framework where job one is producing interpretations of texts, class essays that can then be exchanged for a good grade if they are executed well. Which of course tends to downplay or erase the fact that the theories themselves—feminism, deconstruction, critical race theory—are highly charged sociopolitical engagements that are supposed to perform biopolitical work "on" the students doing the critiquing (rather than paradigms merely working "for" students, allowing them to demonstrate disciplinary mastery).

Just as a practical matter, to foreground this sense of theory as a transformation engine rather than a series of hermeneutic templates, I have for the past 20 years been arranging my theory survey course (or what's left of it, enrollments have been dropping steadily) around transformative concepts rather than seemingly stagnant schools; so we open with a consideration of differing ways that language *creates* rather than merely *refers*—looking at Saussure, Heidegger, Nietzsche, and Austin. And from there we examine *not* a series of theoretical schools or movements, but a series of concepts taken up and deployed by theorists: authority, subjectivity, reading, gender, race, class, postcolonialism, periodization, the culture industry, and so on. (That's in general also my approach the Sophomore Intro to Theory course, a template laid out in *The Theory Toolbox*, an introductory textbook that I co-authored with Susan Searls Giroux.)

It seems to me that the theory course, hopefully in the past but certainly going forward, is not primarily undertaken in the name of teaching core disciplinary content ("This is what a deconstruction of a Wallace Stevens poem looks like; here's what a feminist reading of the same poem looks like"); rather, theory is a biopolitical transformation tool, and the students themselves—those who can combine and create concepts if given the right tools and vocabulary—are the course's outcome, not whether anybody remembers the ins and outs of Saussure's synchronic critique of historical linguistics and its origin myths. In short, it seems to me that theory is a way of life, not a menu of methods.

But what can that mean—theory is a biopolitical way of life to be enacted, not primarily a disciplinary content to be mastered? How am I understanding biopolitics in its distinction from discipline? In his 1979 *Birth of Biopolitics* lecture series, Michel Foucault revisits Adam Smith to thematize the changes wrought from Smith's liberal era of classical capitalism to the neoliberal intensifications that were just beginning in the Thatcher–Reagan–Kohl era. Where for Smith the subject of disciplinary capitalism was the person of consumption as exchange (understood as a partner in a mutually beneficial transaction of preexisting goods or commodities—"fair trade"), Foucault argues that the biopolitical subject is a person of production, one who's constantly (re)producing herself through desiring investments. Smith's version of liberalism, in other words, hopes to produce a "disciplinary" intervention on the subject (in Foucault's parlance, it "acts upon actions," hoping to increase docility by more intense suturing to a system), while neoliberalism's homo economicus is a harbinger of Foucaultian biopower, someone whose "life" and "identity" is under constant re- and deconstruction (rather than the fixed or molded subject that constitutes discipline's bearing area—wherein you're trained to fulfill a role through your identity: soldier, mother, teacher, student, citizen, and so on).

To relocate that larger drama of disciplinary versus biopolitical subjectivity narrowly into the terms of the undergraduate theory course, faculty who teach such courses remain, I think, by and large captivated by Foucault's first (liberal or disciplinary) version of the subject (which emphasizes deliberation, consensus, and discursive understanding as a mutually beneficial understanding of classroom citizenship), whereas our students are not engaging primarily in that drama: they're biopolitical (or even neoliberal) subjects, who are looking to increase their shares of a slippery thing called "life." They're first and foremost libidinal investors, in the broad senses of both those words, in their own developing subjectivities. While we faculty members tend to think of ourselves as disciplinary stewards—and if we're selling anything at all in the classroom (already a contentious thought for many academics), it's knowledge, and such disciplinary knowledge isn't primarily the gear oil of an open-ended biopolitical production machine. Rather, disciplinary knowledge is akin to AAA-rated bonds (a gourmet menu of proven dishes—Plato, Freud, DuBois, and the like). Ironically, in that way the theory survey's understanding of knowledge—say, being able to recognize (or even write) a new historicist reading of "The Yellow Wallpaper"—is much more about consumption than it is about production: which is to say, assigning or producing such an essay begs the question of why anyone would want to new historicize Charlotte Perkins Gilman in the first place, or what difference it makes.

Or just think about the biopolitics of the contemporary theory classroom this way: students, when asked what they like or remember about the course, almost never refer to the course content—I learned a lot about the history of literary theory. Students like a course when, say it with me, "I learned a lot about myself"—which is to say, students like a course when they have accrued something that they can use in their primary job under biopolitical regimes, reinventing their lives through consistent production and reproduction of their identity. In this way, students are not exactly consumers (the lament we hear consistently), but they are prosumers—who through their consumption of "college" end up producing only one product: their subjectivity. Ok, two products: their subjectivity and a mountain of debt—though that's a topic for another book.

In a panic (and there's been more than enough panic going around in the humanities these days), it's too easy to fall back on the transmission of

tried-and-true disciplinary model of what we do in and around the literature department. When you ask my colleagues, just by way of an example,
why students need required courses in the history of literature, they initially
seem shocked that anyone would ask, then go on to give a resolutely disciplinary series of answers: because without understanding Victorian British
literature you'll never see what's unique about modernism, for example, or
that any educated English major needs to know something about Chaucer
and Shakespeare, and so on. I won't dispute the veracity of these claims,
but I will point out they have zero biopolitical uptake with students—they're
merely disciplinary answers, and our students don't think of themselves as
disciplinary subjects, in need of a developing story about the content of $x$ or $y$
subdiscipline, whether it be early modern English literature or contemporary
literary theory.

Theory of course has an advantage over literary history here in the
biopolitical present: feminist psychoanalysis or critical race theory are less sets
of texts to be mastered or tools to be deployed in interpreting texts than they
are flexible sets of practices and problematics that can be put into productive
resonance, or not, with a wide range of cultural objects, not all of them (nor
maybe even most of them) literary in nature, and thereby not really in need
of an individually produced "interpretation." Indeed, this seems to me why
something like theory is in a much better position than literature to survive
the exodus of students from the literature classroom. And just in a passing
sideways glance from my sense that that theory is a way of life (not a list of
methods), I'm not so sure one could say just as easily that "literature is a way
of life," unless by that you mean creative writing (producing literature); and
maybe that's the current crisis of the literature major in a nutshell: familiarity
with a list of privileged disciplinary objects does not necessarily constitute a
valuable course of study in the twenty-first century.

In regard to that breakdown or splintering of the canon, I've heard it said
over the years that theory thereby killed the study of literature—that the hermeneutics of suspicion ruined the appreciation of literary mastery, and it was
all downhill from there. Take, for example, the critique offered by my former
colleague Wendell Harris in his 1996 book *Literary Meaning: Reclaiming the Study
of Literature*: "Literary theory [...] has over the last twenty-five years become
increasingly characterized by illogical arguments, an esoteric vocabulary, and
gnomic references to what various authority figures are presumed to have
demonstrated. Arcane modes of argument and unargued assumptions leave
the reader of contemporary theorists frustrated; little of the resulting criticism
entices the reader to seek out the literary work itself."[14] While I see a lot of
myself in the target of this argument, though Wendell was always very nice to
me as a junior faculty member, I'd have to say respectfully that the situation

seems to me exactly the opposite: theory didn't kill "the study of literature" but far rather extended literature's academic life considerably by giving this resolutely analog form another quarter-century of disciplinary centrality in a world that had long since gone digital. (And of course one might note that Harris's position is finally yet another "theory," rather than the overcoming or dismissal thereof.) However you slice it, and whatever your theoretical orientation, the arcane intricacies of theory have proven to be very, very good for academic literary study over the past 50 years—you can only sponsor so many journals or publish so many books where people endlessly fight over the real or plain "literary meaning" of *The Sound and the Fury* (as if such a thing actually existed). But if you're going to take the text seriously, sooner or later you've got to broaden the discussion to the presence or absence of serious reflection on race in Faulkner, examinations of gender dynamics in the text, what it might have to say about disability, various parallel historical concerns, the role of capitalism in and around the narrative, and so on. In any case, going forward I don't so much fear for the future of theory—as I take theory to be a robust set of engagements with the world, a set of flexible questions and practices rather than a series of templates for producing interpretations. About literature, at least literature understood as a series of privileged objects that one is required to read and appreciate to maintain disciplinary coherence, I have very serious doubts.

It's worth noting as well that naysayers have long been enamored of declaring the death of theory, or at least the death of this or that theory. (The disciplinary history of theory may in fact be nothing other than a series of such pronouncements.). However, I've not seen many people over the years worrying over the death of literature itself as an area of academic endeavor. In most discussions, it has seemed as if the centrality of literature is safe and enduring, while the primary ongoing worries concern the shifting theoretical tools necessary to access or talk about literature with new generations of colleagues, administrators, and students. Even the English Department's response to the Black Lives Matter protests—with commitments to diversify the faculty and the literature curriculum or to admit more Black Studies graduate students—tends to elide the larger question: What if, alongside the academic job market in English, literature itself is in the midst of an extinction event? If you think of theory as a way of life, the ruthless rethinking of all that is, then it's all of a piece, as a kind of life hack. (And likewise, once you think you've got it worked out, theory shows you that wrong you are.) The theory survey could be a course that introduces students to a toolbox of (self-)transformation—techniques and zones of potential inquiry, modes of response to the world. The value or aim of such a course might not be mastery of schools or methods of textual interpretation, nor an introduction to a menu of possible methods to consume, but putting on offer a flexible series of recipes or practices to experiment with.

Whereas the study of literature, understood as a series of neo-canonical historical objects that constitute together a discipline, is and for some time has been a pipe dream: no matter how many required courses and aesthetic masterpieces you pile on them, students these days will never imbibe the "Beowulf to Virginia Woolf" story intact. And that anti- or post-disciplinary fact is probably one of the only things still keeping students coming into the major. But at the end of the day, it's probably wishful thinking for me to assert (even though I nevertheless will do so at the end of this book) that theory is the "dog" of English departments, and literature is merely the wagging "tail," when functionally of course it remains the opposite: the status and effectiveness of literary theory and methodology as a field is, by definition, subordinated to the status of literature and its continuing worth and centrality. What I will insist upon here, however, is that any definition of "literature" (both its historical objects and its various forms) is never realized by locating anything intrinsic within a given set of texts, but rather by a prior theoretical intervention that pinpoints what might qualify as "literariness" among those texts; and as such, a theory thereby reveals their status and importance: Anne Frank's diaries or Jonathan Edwards's Puritan sermons aren't "literary" until a founding theoretical intervention locates them as such.

As Foucault reminds us, disciplines don't *find* their objects and privileged authors; rather, disciplines *produce* such objects and authors through differing theoretical "ways of handling texts."[15] So, for example, Melville becomes one of the greatest American writers of the nineteenth century only in the twentieth century, with the rise of new critical symbol-hunting and the larger pedagogical postwar push to use the history of American literature to bolster individualist democratic values. For both of those projects, something like the highly metaphor-laden anti-authoritarianism of *Moby-Dick* is a kind of proof text—or at least it was for the book that largely "rediscovered" Melville, F. O. Matthiessen's 1941 *American Renaissance: Art and Expression in the Age of Emerson and Whitman*. In any case, the point is this: there are no ready-made disciplinary objects without the prior intervention of a theoretical paradigm, because the theory indicates what to look for and what to value (e.g., Matthiessen's art as "expression") in and among the vast sea of available texts that might be studied closely in an any given period, for example the "age of Emerson and Whitman" (which could just as easily be dubbed the "age of Douglass and Stowe," but that book would be driven by a different set of theoretical paradigms concerning how and why literature matters). To put it another way, disciplines don't run on foundational answers—"We in theology have finally figured out what God is!"—but rather on developing questions, approaches, and hesitations: disciplines work through structural and enabling attempts that try to (re)define or (re)position their objects in the present ("The Economics of Bitcoin" or "The Dutch Tulip Mania, Reconsidered"), rather than attempts to answer their foundational questions once and for all ("Economists Finally Reveal the True Nature of Value").

So we return again to that basic issue for literary study: how does literature function, today? While on the whole within English departments there is a great deal of common ground surrounding literary studies' value and some disagreement (mostly between those who feel that literature is a discipline of historically connected books/ideas and those who think it's a biopolitical exercise in teaching sensitivity toward other points of view and ways of life), consistently elided remains the most foundational question of all: what exactly is literature good for, today, in the United Biopolitical States of America? Even the Clune versus Dettmar–Starr debate takes on this question concerning literature in a necessarily indirect way—which is to say, each of them finally treats the question of literature as a question of methodological approach. For Clune, the judgment schooled by literary discipline is anti-neoliberal, against the false equivalency of all responses, and that's why it's useful; while for Detmarr and Starr literature is good at introducing us to multiple empathetic points of view.

But at either pole of this argumentative disagreement, which is really a theoretical disagreement rather than a literary one, it's nearly impossible to argue that literature as it has been traditionally defined (especially the pre-twentieth-century British and American literature that's such a large part of English's portfolio) is a privileged, unique, or even appropriate modality of either anti-capitalist aesthetic critique or empathy training: English and American literature would, by definition, be one thing among many, many others in a broader ethical or political project, wherein literature might (and probably should) easily be replaced by more accessible and useful content—say, film and video or popular music. *Paradise Lost* might be good for all kinds of things in terms of old-fashioned disciplinary imperatives concerning poetic form, philological reference, and aesthetic judgment, but it doesn't immediately lend itself to anti-neoliberal critique nor toward fostering sympathy for multiple points of view. However, virtually any painting by Barbara Kruger or any song recorded by rap duo Run the Jewels will do both of those things quite handily.

In short, if you read around in these ubiquitous articles on the "crisis of literary study," there's no clear consensus on the answer to the question, "what, specifically, is literature itself good for today?" Perhaps the thing to note more forcefully is that most authors who work in universities don't even raise this fundamental question—they're too busy trying to beat back the wolves from the door. But the question is worth insisting on: we know why students say "no" to an English major (or we think we know). But when those brave students say "yes" to becoming an English major, what exactly are they affirming? And any answer to that question can only be given in terms of theoretical paradigm.

Which brings us back to another sense of "elegy" that will occupy us in the following chapter, organized around a question that's well-nigh heresy if you ask it in the English department mail room: is there something about literature itself, as it's presently understood and functions culturally, that no longer draws people or serves as a driver of anything much culturally? Do we professors of literature even still believe, deep down, that today literature is a linchpin for anything in particular, in terms of cultural centrality? Most everyone in the elegiac crisis mode suggests that the academic study of literature was severely wounded by the exterior economics of the 2008 financial crisis, and then the upheavals of 2020 will have come along to give academic administrators enough cover to finish the job of assassinating literature departments; as my English Department colleague and former Modern Language Association president Michael Bérubé sums up the collective angst concerning "The Future of the Academic Work Force," "I am not sure how we recover from this. It is looking more and more like an extinction event."[16]

But what if it's less a Chicxulub situation, extinction by unforeseen meteor, and more that the academic literary study has been dying a kind of death from other, I hesitate to call them "natural" precisely because they're historical and theoretical, causes for some time now? Why does literature as living cultural form matter, today and going forward? What theoretical paradigm or paradigms can foreground or explain the cultural necessity of literature in the historical present? This question seems to me to be stubbornly elided in almost all academic literary criticism today. For example, the myriad discussions of those shiny new modes of adjectival reading that are supposedly going to reinvigorate academic literary criticism—post-critical reading, distant reading, surface reading, descriptive reading, reparative reading, and so on—take it for granted that the cultural centrality of the literary object is as secure as the rock of Gibraltar; the only question remains how we choose innovatively to "read" it going forward. As if to question the centrality of literature, or the project of literary interpretation, would be blasphemy on the face of it. But even if we assume it's true that literature no longer occupies a pivotal position within contemporary aesthetic experience, nor is it the undisputed backbone of the humanities curriculum, that would hardly be synonymous with admitting that studying literature is worthless: precious few of the people who dedicate their academic lives to the studying of Sanskrit grammar or ancient Chinese history think that those disciplines contain any obvious relevance or easy translation to twenty-first century American social life and its problems, or that their research areas should be the undisputed core of the contemporary humanities curriculum. So why do we or should we continue to think, again, however silently, that the history (or the present, for that matter) of English and American literature has any more central educational relevance today?

## Literature—What *Was* It Good For (in the United States, 1945–90)?

Rather than diving directly into that thorny speculative question about the messy present and the uncertain future of literary study, maybe we should start with a prior question concerning literature's recent past: it's easy enough to see, for cultural heritage reasons, the theoretical explanation for why all along Chaucer or Shakespeare (not to mention Dante or Homer) were important for Western civilization curricula, though there the pedagogical emphasis wasn't really on a student's individual interpretation of these texts, in class discussions or written essays, but using those literary texts to provide historical context and continuity for the history of Western culture. But what was reading literature as an English major good for in that previous, presumably golden era (approximately 1945–90) before the major fell into crisis in the United States? That's an easier question to answer, because the very idea that anyone would study contemporary literature in an American university, or that students would learn primarily to "interpret literature for themselves," was a relatively late invention: in the United States the idea that contemporary American literature was worthy of college-level study was first brought to institutional fruition by Fred Lewis Pattee at Penn State, in the early twentieth century (Pattee retired in 1928). So the idea that professors would assign students to read roughly contemporary American literature in college, and talk about its "meaning," is not as old as the hills, but has in fact only been in place for around 100 years. As my friend Ralph Johnson, emeritus Classics professor from the University of Chicago, used to jokingly put it: "Why would any American students need help reading American literature? Don't they know the language?" So when it comes to the collegiate study of contemporary literature, we'd do well to remember right out of the gate what Foucault urges us to remember about the category of "man"—it's "an invention of recent date, and one perhaps nearing its end."[17]

In any case, that project of students analyzing literature in order to come up with their own interpretation ("reading" literature to uncover its "meaning") would almost certainly have remained a very small part of the American university portfolio, and American universities (especially the now-enormous state schools) would have remained much smaller operations on the whole, were it not for a single world-historical event: the Second World War. As the US armed forces shipped American young men off to Europe and the Pacific, women and still-segregated minorities became larger parts of the stateside work force. And once the war is over, millions of working-class men return home triumphant, but for many there's not much to do (their jobs having been absorbed). Cue the GI Bill, in which the government will pay for you to go to college if you went to war—which was of course part of the payback for the lower and middle classes who actually fought, but were not previously thought of as college material. Combine the GI Bill with the fact that after the hot war with the Nazis, there was a new Cold War with the Russians, and this was to be both a tech war and a culture war (remember "hearts and minds"?) for global dominance—communism versus capitalism—so it was all hands on deck. In short, education was seen as a key component of that larger ideological war with communism. In the newly minted age of nuclear weapons and mutually assured destruction, we were going to have to outthink, rather than simply outfight, our enemy the Red Menace; and as implausible as it sounds, it's in that context specifically that reading literature becomes a cornerstone of K–12 American education in the United States, and a key component of college curricula after the war.

This central place for literature in American education is laid out in the highly influential 1945 Harvard-sponsored planning document, *General Education in a Free Society*, the so-called Redbook. For the sculptors of Cold War general education, teaching students to interpret literature was part of a strategy for building a citizenry that could out-innovate and outthink the Russians and other communists (who are, in the Redbook's terms, precisely not "free" to think for themselves). That well-rounded individual, who could decide for himself (and the masculine pronoun is deliberate here), was to be America's ticket to defeating communism—or at least defeating a rigid parody of Marxism that stresses, on a jaundiced 1945 understanding, obedience to dogma, party and authority, and doesn't prize the distinctly American trait of thinking outside the box. Communism doesn't prize the creative individual, to put it in a stereotypical nutshell, and American education of the Cold War period was to be dedicated to sculpting just those (antinomian) individuals. And their authenticity as free individuals finds a central outlet in learning to interpret literature.

Geoffrey Galt Harpham puts it succinctly in his authoritative work on the mid-century rise of literary studies in the United States:

> The driving force behind the concretization of the humanities after the war was almost nakedly strategic and political—the desire to strengthen the American nation by producing citizens capable of the confident exercise of the freedoms available in, and protected by, a modern democratic culture. [...] Liberal education, in the form of what the "Redbook"

produced at Harvard in 1945 called "general education," advanced the idea that learning experiences ought to be conducted in a spirit of free inquiry without regard to vocational or professional utility. According to the authors of the Redbook, the humanities were to be the heart and soul of general education, a moral kernel in colleges and universities, whose overall mission was to produce virtuous, cultivated, responsible, and well-rounded individuals.[18]

As Harpham makes clear, it was refining this brand of free, against-the-herd individuality that was entrusted to the humanities in the Cold War era, and that task was specifically tethered to the central project of an individual student's interpretation of literary works: "It is the exceptionally high and repeatedly affirmed value placed by Americans on the right to one's own opinion that is ultimately responsible for the elevation of what became known as the humanities, as well as for the prominence of the discipline of English in the American system."[19] In short, and in direct response to the question "what was literature good for from 1945 until around 1989 (when the cold war ended with the fall of the Berlin Wall)?," one could answer that literature was important to American education, from the ground up, as part of a Cold War nation-building (which is to say, subject-building) strategy, firmly directed against collectivist communism. The study of literature, specifically in terms of individual students producing their own interpretations of texts, was a central educational apparatus for producing this new, free, and individualistic American.

But to get masses of students geared up to interpret literature "for themselves," there also needed to be something of a theoretical paradigm shift in literary critical methods, away from the largely philological, historicist, or biographical understandings of texts that had ruled university literature curricula before the Second World War. And so rises to dominance the central paradigm for thinking about literature in the early to mid-twentieth-century, new criticism, which is tailor-made for the post–GI Bill influx of new students, precious few of whom know Greek or Latin, or much about history, so the old philological and historical studies simply won't work with this new population of students. Instead you plunk these new students down, in front of either classic or contemporary literature, and teach them to look for metaphor, irony, paradox, character motivation, mood, universal themes—all that good stuff for which students don't need any preexisting aesthetic abilities or historical context. Students schooled in the new criticism are in fact strictly forbidden to speculate about anything outside the text. In short, new criticism, the dominant literary theory from the 1940s–70s, worked hand in glove with the influx of new kinds of students into the university classroom, and found itself equally suited for the postwar baby boom in K–12 education—the institutional realization of what John Crowe Ransom had called for in his 1937 essay "Criticism Inc."[20]

The postwar triumph of new criticism is maybe not surprising, as prominent new critic I. A. Richards was among the architects of the Harvard Redbook and the one who wrote the (admittedly strange) section on literature, which leaves little to chance in its directives concerning what's to be avoided when teaching literature to these free American citizens. Those of us familiar with new criticism, and its axiomatic divorce of the literary text from any references supposedly outside it, will recognize immediately its foregrounding in the Redbook's language: "Among prevailing trends to be discouraged in the study of literature," the Redbook lists the following approaches to be avoided at all costs:

Stress on factual content as divorced from design.
Emphasis on literary history, on generalizations as to periods, tendencies and
    ready-made valuations in place of deeper familiarity with the texts.
Strained correlation with civics, social studies.
Overambitious technical analysis of structure, plot, figurative language,
    prosody, genre.
Use of critical terms (Romanticism, Realism, Classical, Sentimental) as tags,
    coming between the reader and the work.
Didacticism: lessons in behavior too closely sought.[21]

Once you carefully avoid emphasis on a work's content, its literary history or political concerns, or it being merely representative of a literary movement or school, and you dispense with the notion that the work contains some handy moral to take away, Richards's section of the Redbook turns its attention to where literary critical emphasis *should* properly reside. The lesson continues,

As means to developing better reading, stress is to be laid:

On intensive, close study of well-written paragraphs and poems which are saying important things compactly.

On what a word is doing in a place on a page in addition to its dictionary sense and the dependence of this upon the context.

On the normal ingredients of full meaning: the literal sense, the metaphoric implications, the writer's (or speaker's) mood, his tone, his intent, his attitudes toward his point, his reader, himself, his work, and other people and things.

On the utility, almost the necessity, of metaphor; and the fruitfulness of intensive imaginative study of how the mind relies on parallels in all its doings.[22]

On such a rendering of the literary work's importance, all that students require for a healthy general education in the "free," new critical interpretation of literature is a couple of hints concerning what to look for in any given text: the primary concern at all points is the question of internal literary forms and figures—metaphor, paradox, irony, ambiguity, character or speaker motivation, and themes. And on the Redbook's rendering, the student will likewise require considerable advice concerning what not to do when interpreting a text. Certainly do not merely paraphrase the work's factual content—"Uhh, it's about a wet red wheelbarrow next to some chickens" or "it's about trying to catch a big white whale." Nor should the student venture "outside" the text to find an interpretation grounded in history, politics, comparative morality, or representative literary or social movements—"Uhh, it's an example of modernist imagism" or "it's about resistance to global capitalism and the beginnings of the environmental movement." Meaning, in a free society, is to be found in the text, and nothing but the text.

Reduced to these teachable bullet points, new criticism was tailor-made for instructing generations of students who had no prior knowledge about, or facility in, other modes for making sense of texts (chasing down allusions to classical texts, philology, linguistics, knowledge of historical, political, or genre parallels). The questions aren't about what allusions Shakespeare is making here, where his language come from, how much he is like or unlike his contemporary dramatists, and certainly not how is he commenting on contemporary politics. The question is simply, what does the text mean—or, better, how does it evoke the paradoxical and ironic plethora of meanings that we can mine from within any of the "great" texts? (Why literature for the new critics is not to be confused with a memo or an editorial—it contains multiple, shifting layers of meaning.)

And this new critical apparatus decisively produced and institutionalized its preferred literary canon through the tireless work of one central figure, Cornell professor M. H. Abrams, who was the driving force behind *The Norton Anthology of English Literature*, and its principal editor from the first edition in 1962 through its seventh in 2006. It would be hard indeed to overestimate the scope and influence of this single (though of course massive) volume: Sean Shesgreen calls the *Norton Anthology of English Literature* "a book on which the whole profession of English letters depends, especially in America."[23] Shesgreen's short inside history of Abrams and the *Norton Anthology*, "Canonizing the Canonizer," demonstrates the massive influence that Abrams exercised over the theory and practice of literary studies throughout the latter part of the twentieth century (the boom years) and into the twenty-first century (when the *Anthology* was forced to diversify its offerings in the face of a series of multicultural competitors cutting into its market share). For our purposes, however, the most important piece of this story is that Abrams' mentor and postgraduate tutor at Cambridge was none other than I. A. Richards, giving us a strong throughline from the Harvard Redbook's influence in the 1940s and 1950s to the *Norton Anthology's* solidification and continuation of those new critical principles from the 1960s forward in the United States, at least until the canon wars of the 1990s.

New criticism's theoretical vocabulary offers interpretive tools, and those tools themselves—what you're looking for when you look at a piece of literature—produce a tightly controlled canon of "great" writers; as Abrams confessed in 2004, while he was being forced to add women writers to his *Anthology*, "I have not found ten lines worth reading in any of the women added."[24] But as important as "great texts" are for the new critical role of literature in the classroom, it all comes down to deploying that vocabulary within a highly individuated reading encounter with those texts—and in the context of the Cold War, such individuation encapsulates the "free" American alternative to Soviet collectivity. It all comes down to the question, "What do you think about Hemingway's 'The Killers,' Billy?" And needless to say, such student encounters with individual texts are likewise perfect for the supposedly meritocratic demands of teaching and grading: if Billy can find the overarching theme in Hemingway's story (heroism? despair? the heroism of accepting despair?), he gets an A. If the person sitting next to Billy—say, Jane—can't find these overarching themes, or offers to the class that she thinks Hemingway is just a litany of puerile, toxic examples of white masculinity masquerading as universal human experience, then Jane gets a C.

In determining the supposed "success" of any given literary interpretation in the Cold War period, the apolitical, atomized individualism of new criticism is hardly a problem or a bug in the system, but is rather a critical piece of the programming for the mid- to late twntieth-century project of building "free" Americans. In any case, love it or hate it, new criticism took the literary hermeneutics and made it into a flexible and growing profession, rather than a kind of backyard or book-club conversation. That individualized interpretive encounter with the text only intensified through the theory years—deconstruction, new historicism, feminism, Marxism, up to and including contemporary post-critique: these theory revolutions certainly changed decisively where one might look for this elusive thing called literary meaning. Even though most of these new paradigms ventured beyond the closed formalist text that was new criticism's sole object of study, they nonetheless remained for the most

part interpretive paradigms built on producing clever new readings of texts
(thereby more like new criticism than radically unlike it). In the classroom,
there were more "acceptable" pedagogical questions—and student answers—
concerning Joseph Conrad's *Heart of Darkness* in 1985 than there were in 1945,
but those questions and answers remained largely territorialized on the story's
"meaning," and thereby in essence remained "new critical" questions (even if
the interpretive answers were informed by decidedly worldly movements like
postcolonial theory).

Of course, the Cold War was over by 1990, with free market capitalism
having "triumphed." At that point, however, the university (and general education as a whole) in the United States no longer needed to continue funding
the ideological project of creative subject making to counter the anti-con-
sumerist collectivism of Reds. And within the university literature department, the new criticism and its understanding of texts had been under attack
for a few decades by a host of emergent "extra-textual" methodologies for
producing literary meaning. New criticism was called out for its faux (white
male) tropes of universality, and its somewhat jaundiced understanding of
literature as radically divorced from the sociopolitical world. That theory
moment of the 1970s and 1980s constituted a temporary boom for university
literary study, as it offered literary scholars a whole bunch of new things to
say about old texts (deconstructionist, feminist, Marxist, new historicist, ethnic
or race-based readings of canonical works), and a whole bunch of new texts
to say new things about (the canon wars that introduced new texts written by
women, working-class writers, and authors of color).

That theory moment within the American university, after the Cold War
and after the new criticism, then trickles down from universities into K–12 literary pedagogy—where curricula are no longer fetishizing the interior form
of texts, or even really clever new interpretations, but have come to pivot
instead on texts' sociopolitical import: in high school in 2018, for example, my
son was assigned to read Chinua Achebe's *Things Fall Apart*, but the teacher
merely summarized *Heart of Darkness* for the students (after admitting that
she'd never read Conrad's novella either—at least partially because of the
contemporary settled law that it's racist). Couple those sociopolitical aspects
coming to the forefront in literary studies with the fact that we're no longer in
need of Western universals and individual taste making in order to produce
citizens ready to beat the Reds in the global war for hearts and minds, and we
can see how dramatically the educational function of literature has changed
over the past 30 years. No longer the individualist interpretive linchpin of the
entire humanities, performing its job one of creating well-rounded Westerners
whose cultured individualism can help us outflank the herd mentality of communism, literature in the present remains without a central or defining role in

American education. Which is to say, at present there is no widely accepted theory that could decisively locate literature as central to contemporary American cultural (and/or subject) production.

## Regimes of (Ir)Relevance

As Galen Tihanov phrases a parallel genealogical point in his provocative *The Birth and Death of Literary Theory*,[25] the heyday of literature was likewise the heyday of literary theory in the academy, from the formalists (in Russia, then the United States) in the early twentieth century right up through the deconstruction years. What Tihanov calls the "regime of relevance" that obtained for literature in those years was ruled over by the "idea of the autonomy of literature" (20) first birthed in Romanticism's absolute privilege of the author's aesthetic expression, and later morphing into the autonomy of the text itself (the autonomy of language, rather than the writer's expressive verve) in the hermeneutic theories of the twentieth century: the Romantics' "early version of the autonomy of literature inaugurated a new regime of relevance, preparing the ground for the Formalist account: literature's relevance does indeed reside in its uniqueness, but that uniqueness cannot be derived from the exclusive social position of the writer; rather it must be located in the special way in which language is deployed in literature" (20). From a nineteenth-century Romantic "regime of relevance" where literature's power is guaranteed by the genius of the author, Thainov notes a shift in literature's regime of relevance born with twentieth century's modernist and postmodernist aesthetics and their links to formalist criticism, which looks away from the author to focus on the linguistic autonomy of the text.

From there, Thianov goes on to argue that we've seen over the past three decades what he calls "the transition to a third regime of relevance, where literature is increasingly recognized not for its [aesthetically autonomous] social and political weight, nor indeed for some presumed uniqueness, but, in a rather low-key way, for the (largely individual) entertainment and therapy it can provide" (23) to a reader—a transition of relevance regimes for literature that, on his account, "overlaps with the freshly transfigured regime of some direct social relevance exemplified in the struggles of 'identity politics' and the battles over 'representative' minority, national, and global canons" (24). I take Thianov here to be less lamenting literature's fall from (universalist white male) grace than describing both a social and theoretical shift in literature's function, both inside and outside the academy. Precious few critics, and even fewer general readers, these days would insist on the formalist autonomy of the text and its linguistic avant-garde innovations, nor radically want to divorce any given literary work from the author and his, her, or their own-voiced, autofictive experience. The disciplinary apparatus of literature and literary criticism, one might say, has given way to the biopolitics of affective reader interest—and to bolster this point within the academy, one could gesture again toward those several strands of "post-critical" reading strategies that depend on affective biopolitical responses rather than "suspicious" disciplinary critique.

In thinking about literature in the present, Tihanov suggests, we've arrived at the polar opposite of the modernist, disciplinary dream of banishing the author in order to focus solely on the text's linguistic autonomy (think of the hermeneutic trajectory running from Wimsatt and Beardsley's new critical "The Authorial Fallacy" through Barthes's post-structuralist "Death of the Author" all the way to Foucault's genealogical account in "What is an Author?", and its famous redeployment of Beckett's question, "What does it matter who's speaking?"). Today, in a biopolitical sense, it makes all the difference in the world who's speaking, insofar as our contemporary regime of relevance—what Foucault would call our "mode of veridiction"—holds that literature can no longer speak for itself, or no longer speaks in the voice of noninterested, normative disciplinary linguistic authority. Biopolitically, autofictive or own-voiced literature necessarily speaks for and from a life, or else it can't—or at least shouldn't, as we saw in the controversy surrounding Jeanine Cummins' *American Dirt*—speak at all.

Of course you can always decry this new biopolitical regime of relevance as a neoliberal dystopia, rule by Twitter mob, politically correct identity politics, or the coddling of the American mind; but in a larger sense what you see here is neither the wholesale abandonment of norms nor a return to premodernist or Romantic modes of literary value, but a decisively changed relation between what counts as literary "knowledge" and its "mode of veridiction" in the twenty-first century. The erosion of disciplines and the concomitant triumph of biopolitics forges a new knowledge connection in literature between an author and literary value—which is not a regression to a regime of relevance that emphasizes Byronic genius, exactly, but a matter of the work's having an anchor in the author's own lived experience, which constitutes an essential twenty-first century link to literary value.

Insofar as the modernist project of "making it new" does continue apace, it's forwarded these days less in and through literature than it is by social media and attention-grabbing advertising. As David Antin puts it in "what it means to be avant-garde," "practically every role classically/attributed to the avant-garde has been preempted by something/else"[26] today, so it seems that literature has had to find a new job in the twenty-first century. Or if nothing else, Mary Oliver's oft-repeated mantra for thinking about literature's relation to everyday life—"Pay attention/Be Astonished/Tell about it"[27]—could just as easily function as the slogan for clickbait social media sites like Twitter and

Facebook. In any case, switching career paths from "make it new" to "make it entertaining and authentically ownvoiced" seems maybe like a larger cultural "win" to gain general readers (it's not clear how many readers postmodern behemoths like *Gravity's Rainbow* or *Infinite Jest* actually had, though in general the reading of fiction is way, way down over the past decades); but such a mutation in literature's raison d'etre hardly seems like an advance for the academic study of literature, or even a lateral move. Who wants to major in literary studies if reading deeply in the history of English and American literature has become essentially a hobby—and a retrograde, frankly neo-racist one at that? This, it seems to me, is the unacknowledged elephant in the room at the English department meeting today.

# Chapter 2

# THE NOVEL AND NEW MATERIALISM; OR, LEARNING FROM LUKÁCS

*—Shall I project a world?*

—Oedipa Maas, *The Crying of Lot 49*[1]

Let me begin this chapter by recalling an anecdote from 2019's MLA Convention in Chicago, specifically a session sponsored by the forum for philosophy and literature. That panel was dedicated to the question of "Extinction," and Branka Arsić gave a particularly fascinating talk on Melville's whales. It was a great paper, but I had to ask in the Q&A: "I realize that we're here at a literature convention, and if this were a panel on extinction at a plumbers' convention, we would certainly be talking about extinction in terms of plumbing. But otherwise I honestly can't see why any particular novel, even one as great as *Moby-Dick*, matters in this case, why literature specifically or centrally matters to the questions of animality, posthumanism, climate change, or the 6th great extinction event that we're presently living through?" (And in a world where 4.2 billion people, more than half the world's human population, presently live without safely managed sanitation, those questions are undoubtedly more urgently being posed at plumbers' conventions.) However, someone from behind me immediately retorted, in I guess a Lyotardian or de Manian vein, "What leads you to believe that literature isn't already the inhuman?" I think I responded, "Uhh, because humans are literature's sole producers and consumers: what does the delphinium, the napkin dispenser, or the giant squid care for literature? It's our problem, not theirs."

Professor Arsić's more measured response was, as usual, well thought out and instructive. Of course literature is a human-centric undertaking, she insisted, but literature is especially good at foreground the ethical specificity of any given question. The stakes in literary production are initially human (whales don't read Melville—but then again, neither do many of our human students); but literature also opens us out beyond ourselves, with any luck at all: literature, especially fiction, projects a world that may or may not be centered on humans, and/or allows humans to see themselves as part of a larger mesh that makes up such a multiverse. There's a kind of illocutionary force of language on display in literature that opens it up past the (human) question of meaning, into the realms of alterity. Language is the stuff of literature, but it's the new materialist emphasis on the vibrancy of things (including language), rather than on the linguistic-turn question of human meaning that allows us more clearly to see the inhuman or posthuman force that traverses literature.

As Diana Coole and Samantha Frost write in the introduction to their collection *New Materialisms*, a central tenet of the movement holds that "materiality is always something more than 'mere' matter: an excess, force, vitality, relationality, or difference that renders matter active, self-creative, productive, unpredictable. In sum, new materialists are rediscovering a materiality that materializes, evincing immanent modes of self-transformation."[2] And it is precisely this aesthetically excessive notion of "life" that new materialism wants to export from the exclusive purview of the human, to animate the entirety of matter in the universe. So what's the challenge presented there to modernist and postmodernist aesthetics? Well, once you posit or discover that matter itself is animate, that everything is always already "making it new," then there is no longer a neat binary opposition between "living" matter like humans, animals, and plants (which are self-organizing, world-producing, creative, and striving) and "non-living" matter like rock formations or the earth itself (which were previously thought to be inert, largely unchanging entities). Once it's accepted that matter itself is constantly in flux, then we humans don't any longer have to be burdened with reenchanting or restoring worldly possibility—aesthetically defamiliarizing the reified world of inert objects by bestowing our precious artistic attention in order to add wonder to everyday life. The deterritorializing force of matter runs through us and our language, rather than vice versa; and that perhaps robs literature of its unique, humanist world-disclosing function (wherein literature projects possibility into an otherwise inert world of meaningless matter), but it hardly puts literature out of a job altogether.

That strikes me as being persuasive, a satisfying response to the question of why literature (still) matters in a quantum world of posthumanist new materialism; but I almost never see that insight about the immaterial force of language played out in the books and literary-studies manuscripts that I read for presses and journals, which still remain stubbornly stuck on the question of literary content and meaning (making sense of plot twists and character motivations), while paying hardly any attention at all to the sentence-level "posthuman" vibrancy of language. Over the past few years, for example, I've been reading a lot of books and manuscripts on literature and finance capitalism—all of them, to a one, beginning with some general theoretical worries about the neoliberal present, then moving on to discuss 3 or 4 novels (or 30 or 40 novels, or in the case of Caren Irr's fine book *Toward the Geopolitical Novel*, a full 125); but they're almost always novels, and ones that are either directly or obliquely "about" the topic under consideration—finance capitalism and/or neoliberal biopolitics. All of which leads us to believe that the question of *content* or the level of the novelistic *plot* constitutes the primary bearing areas for literature and its relations to any given social or political question.

I'm more invested here in thinking about the question or the force of form—the forms of the novel, qua novel, and their potentials to say much of anything about the post- or inhuman, beyond the plot-level realm of content. Which is to say that I'm not primarily interested in how Phillip K. Dick's *Do Androids Dream of Electric Sheep?*, for example, intervenes in these debates because it's *about* post- or inhuman life. That seems obvious enough, but it's the literary delivery system itself that I'm interested in here—just as, for the endless stream of books on literature and finance capitalism, if one is going to say that the contemporary novel resists neoliberalism, one would assume that there has to be some reflection of (and push against) said neoliberal capital in the very form of the work itself. Don DeLillo's novels *Cosmopolis* and *Zero K* are about failing finance capitalists, yes—but what does DeLillo's particular rendering of that content on the formal level have to do with regimes of neoliberal finance?

This all perhaps seems a bit old-fashioned, and nebulous, so let me offer a quick example of my question concerning literary form and thematic content in the novelistic present. Looking for a kind of homologous relation between form and content in the American novel, one need only to point to the prior generation of high postmodernism (in addition to DeLillo and Dick, its most famous practitioners also include Thomas Pynchon and David Foster Wallace), and the hand-in-glove relation between the forms of those novels and their primary thematic content, which I guess you could sum up in shorthand as "paranoia." Despite vast differences among the catalogs of these very prolific writers, one might venture that there's a throughline among them compacted within a devilishly simple question: Am I merely projecting meaning or connection into the world, or am I recognizing a significance that's "really" there?

As Pynchon renders it in *The Crying of Lot 49*, the dilemma goes something like this: "Behind the hieroglyphic streets there would either be a transcendent meaning, or only the earth. [...] Another mode of meaning behind the obvious, or none. Either Oedipa in the orbiting of a true paranoia, or a real Tristero. For there either was some Tristero beyond the appearance of the legacy of America, or there was just America."[3] Such a paranoid relation to the world on the level of plot (are the events happening to individual protagonists connected in some meaningful way, organized by a shadowy Tristero, or are they simply random and thereby bereft of hidden significance?) is obviously and immediately doubled on the formal level of the individual sentences: the reader's experience, like Oedipa's, is likewise the experience of a certain paranoia, as each reader of the novel is compelled on every page to keep making word- and sentence-level connections, with the real meaning of it all just out of reach. Both the events depicted in a novel like *The Crying of Lot 49* and the words that render them do not "contain" meaning, so the sentences themselves relentlessly push the reader forward into an uncertain future, where things may or may not come together: a satisfying sense of order might be rendered or sutured at the end of the sentence or the end of the novel, or maybe not. You may, when all is said and done, still be asked endlessly "to await the crying of lot 49."[4]

Certainly the novel can move beyond paranoia on the thematic level—and definitively has—insofar as the American novel has moved beyond that brand of postmodernism's seemingly universalist (really, white male) obsession with epistemological paranoia and hidden meaning, and into the emergent thematic and stylistic cultural dominant of New Sincerity or autofiction. But the more difficult question is this: can the novel, any novel, really push beyond universalist humanism into the posthuman future *as a form, on the level of the sentence and its (necessary) relation to the developing plot?* Which is at least partially to ask, can the novel move beyond the phenomenological (and finally humanist) question of world-projection and its paranoid relation to socially constructed "meaning"? The jury is very much out on that question, as it's not at all clear how the form of the novel as we know it can adapt to the posthuman, new materialist "world" wherein the realist position on vibrant matter—everything is "alive" in some way(s)—has rendered obsolete the social-constructionist, world-forming concerns of postmodernism, where matter was thought to be an inert, mute form (Pynchon's "just America") that either contained some iron determinist significance (known back in the day as "essentialism"), or it was radically neutral material substrate awaiting the inscription of human meaning ("social constructionism"). As Jane Bennett writes in "Systems and Things: On Vital Materialism and Object-Oriented Philosophy," almost all of the emergent post-critical or new materialist paradigms "share a critique of linguistic and social constructivism" and thereby "see the nonhuman turn as a response to an overconfidence about human power that was embedded in the postmodernism of the 1980s and 1990s."[5] Whatever one thinks about that "either/or" essentialist-social construction drama in the present, both the paranoia of world formation and the individual's (in)ability to construct or project such a meaningful world were central to the form and content of the modernist and postmodernist novel in the linguistic-turn era.

But as we in the criticism and theory world move beyond language and the humanist social construction of meaning as the substrate of our collective worldview, to begin trying to move beyond the ravages of the Anthropocene into the posthuman or new materialist "world" of coevolving networks and meshes of life, we're almost forced to ask: whither the novel—which can easily do without the phenomenological thematic *content* of world projection (which is to say, the novel doesn't have to be *about* an individual anxiously projecting a meaningful world, or not)? But the thornier question is, can the novel do without the *form* of world projection? Because it would seem on the face of it that if it's not engaged in the process of projecting a world, on both the individual sentence and the overarching thematic plot level, then it's not a novel. And if the novel is engaged, on the structural level, in linguistically projecting a world, then it's not in a particularly strong position to constitute a linchpin posthumanist or new materialist form.

## Lukács Redux

Georg Lukács's *Theory of the Novel* famously traces the rise of the novel out of the ashes of the premodern forms of epic poetry and tragic drama; so, unlike some critics who suggest that the novel is a nearly transhistorical form that goes as far back as Xenophon,[6] for Lukács to say "modern novel" is merely to say the same thing twice. Summarizing "the idea put forward in *Theory of the Novel*," Lukács writes that

> the problems of the novel form are here the mirror-image of a world gone out of joint. This is why the 'prose' of life is here only a symptom, among many others, of the fact that reality no longer constitutes a favorable soil for art [...] that has nothing more to do with any world of forms that is immanently complete in itself.[7]

In short, for Lukács the novel is the characteristic form for a world gone problematic (which on his account wasn't the case in the premodern era of the epic, a literary form that unfolds in the precapitalist era when the stars and humans, words and deeds, the individual and the collective were supposedly sympatico). Here Lukács follows a pervasive European line of reasoning that posits the premodern world as a continuous whole, a fetishization particularly common to German philosophy of the nineteenth and early twentieth centuries, wherein the epic or tragic world of the Greeks is characterized as a state where "being and destiny are identical" (30) (though we should note that

Lukács already suggests that the supposed perfection of the Greeks is mainly a backformed symptom of modernity's fragmentation). In any case, out of the ashes of the deeds performed by the epic or tragic hero is born the interior dialogue of the narrative, bourgeois, novelistic subject: "We [moderns] have found the only true substance within ourselves: that is why we have to place an unbridgeable chasm between cognition and action, between soul and created structure, between self and world" (34).

Essentially, for Lukács the novel is the official form of the Kantian Copernican Revolution, the tectonic shift from human experience being guided by the stars of destiny to following the inner light of subjectivity, the only thing to which the modern subject has access, even as such (limited) access disallows the decisiveness of bygone eras: "Kant's starry firmament now shines only in the dark night of pure cognition; it no longer lights any solitary wanderer's path (for to be a man in the new world is to be solitary). And the inner light affords evidence of security, or its illusion, only to the wanderer's next step" (36). Unlike the epic, which is also the story of destiny for peoples and collectives, the events of the novel tailor "the fitness of the action to the essential nature of the [individual] subject—the only guide that still remains" (36). In relation to the epic and tragic orders of the Greek world, wherein as Nietzsche put it, "All that exists is just and unjust and equally justified in both,"[8] for Lukács the novel "is a created totality, for the natural unity of the metaphysical spheres has been destroyed forever" (37). In the transition from the epic to the novel, then, we see the transition from the world being revealed in the epic, to the modernist novelistic imperative that aspires to grasp the world according to the categories of the subject—to impose a kind of temporary order on the chaos of the world, rather than to behold and marvel before the existing meaning revealed by nature.

On this line of reasoning concerning modernity's decisive break from the premodern world of starry revelation, which one sees stretching in German thought from Kant to the Romantics through Nietzsche and Simmel all the way to Heidegger (and beyond), ancient Western thought or art doesn't "make" its own categories; rather it derives them from nature. By contrast, modern European thought, starting with Descartes and traveling through Hume to find its apotheosis in Kant, decisively brackets that kind of "dogmatic" realism guided by nature, to derive whatever knowledge it can directly from the subject—wherein it's solely the categories of the subject's experience that are given and shared among humans, not the structure of anything in the world itself.

Whatever one thinks about the historical veracity of this sweeping metastory about modern and premodern European thought, for our purposes here we can simply note that it is demonstrably *not* the case that the individual subject, projecting a world, is the primary pivot of premodern Western thought. And if you substitute "pre-capitalist" for "pre-modern" in this story of Western modernity's subjective fragmentation and alienation, you'll garner an additional nod of discursive agreement, as virtually all Marxists—among whom Lukács in 1919 is not quite yet included—will agree on this point as well: the rise of capitalism alienates workers from nature, the land, the means of production, and ultimately from each other.

And Lukács adds to this consensus his own spin, which specifically concerns the role of the novel in this transformation to modernity: once the human subject and its problematic experience becomes the pivot for everything else, Lukács insists, then the novel becomes the literary form par excellence. By the eighteenth century in Europe, "the epic had to disappear and yield its place to an entirely new form: the novel" (41), a form that is driven by "creative subjectivity" (53), and the modern human predicament of projecting a new world to compensate for the fragmentation of experience and our being exiled from access to the things themselves. As Lukács would have it, the world of the novel "is a world that does not offer itself either as meaning to the aim-seeking subject or as matter, in sensuous immediacy, to the active subject. It is a second nature, and, like nature (first nature), it is determinable only as the embodiment of recognized but senseless necessities and therefore it is incomprehensible, unknowable in its real substance" (62). Which is of course Kant 101—the essence of the real world is bracketed from us, and all we know "about" the world is what we learn by applying our a priori categories to that world: "The novel is the epic of an age in which the extensive totality of life is no longer directly given, in which the immanence of meaning in life has become a problem, yet which still thinks in terms of totality" (56). Of course that produced, rounded whole of the novel remains always fragmentary (it necessarily comes from and is directed at a particular subject's narrative point of view, and thereby is denied access to the realm of the absolute).

In short, "the concealed totality of life" in the novel is not any hidden content extracted from the realm of the real, but the "indication of a form-giving intention" in the narrative voice and point of view. This new shifting totality is projected within the intentionality of the phenomenological subject: "i.e., the search, which is the only way of expressing the subject's recognition that neither objective life nor its relationship to the subject is spontaneously harmonious in itself": "Thus the fundamental form-determining intention of the novel is objectivized as the psychology of the novel's heroes: they are seekers" (60). For Lukács, the novel of course remains a purely formal and temporary "solution" to this inner/outer problem—insofar as the novel can't finally produce the real, pierce the absolute, nor finally solve the problem of the subject's abandonment within a world of meaningless flow; but the novel can compensate for that exile as the privileged artistic form that offers a satisfactory sense of developing order for any given series of unfortunate events that might befall the subject. (Painting or other visual art like sculpture does also offer a sense of order to the subject's gaze out into the world, but that effect is static; a painting's or sculpture's aesthetic shaping doesn't shift or develop like the plot of a novel.)

And at this point, in the movement from Kant to Hegel, from the three Kantian *Critiques* to Hegel's *Phenomenology*, Lukács suggests that the novel also becomes the privileged form not only for the literary arts but also for philosophy. With Hegelian thought, the novel "is transformed into being" (77): "Individuality [...] finds within itself everything that is essential to and that make[s] its life autonomous—even if what it finds can never be a firm possession or the basis of its life, but is an object of search" (78). So Hegel becomes the (novelistic, mobile) truth of Kantian Copernican revolution:

> The immanence of meaning which the form of the novel requires lies in the hero's finding out through experience that a mere glimpse of meaning is the highest that life has to offer, and that this glimpse is the only thing worth the commitment of an entire life, the only thing by which the struggle will have been justified. The process of finding out extends over a lifetime. (80)

Lukács continues on the Hegelian upshot of the Kantian subjective revolution: "The novel form overcomes its 'bad' infinity by recourse to the biographical form. On the one hand, the scope of the world is limited by the scope of the hero's possible experiences and its mass is organized by the orientation of his development towards finding the meaning of life in self-recognition" (81). In the novel as in the *Phenomenology of Spirit*, the events of the everyday, great or small, "acquire life only when they can be directly related to either the life-experiencing interiority of the individual [...] or the observing and creative eye of the artist's subjectivity" (79)—seeking constantly to project a world where things make sense, only to find after long-suffering experience that it is only in the subjective projecting of sense that we find the absolute. The novel in short becomes the template for modern Western bourgeois consciousness: "the structural categories of the novel constitutively coincide with the world as it is today" (93), a chaotic, meaningless jumble that can only be temporarily "rounded" or ordered through a novelistic process of narrative sequencing by an individual. As such a diagnostic history of modern aesthetic forms, Franco Moretti argues that "*Theory of the Novel* belongs to a small circle of masterpieces—Baudelaire's *tableaux*, Flaubert's novels, Manet's paintings,

Ibsen's plays, or, indeed, Weber's last lectures—where the rules of bourgeois existence are at once ineluctable and bankrupt."[9]

Say what you will about Lukács's account of the novel's rise to dominance out of the ashes of the epic,[10] but I would like to zero in on two things for our purposes here. First, his story of the early modern literary and philosophical rise of the alienated bourgeois individual is nearly settled law within the tradition of continental philosophy. As Foucault, hardly one to unreflectively parrot the German idealist tradition, puts the sentiment, "if from the early Middle Ages to the present day the 'adventure' [story] is an account of individuality, the passage from the epic to the novel, from the noble deed to the secret singularity, from long exiles to the internal search for childhood, from combats to phantasies, it is also inscribed in the formation of a disciplinary society."[11] As sweeping as Lukács's story of the novel's rise may seem, it's very widely shared as a canonical explanation for Western modernity, within disparate philosophical traditions from phenomenology through the history of science to Marxism. Following along on that truism, I think it's uncontroversial to say that the philosophical basis upon which Lukács's story stands—Kant to Hegel on the structuring necessity of the human subject—is not exactly where we find ourselves today, in the emergent world of posthumanism and new materialism.

Alongside this central structuring position for the human subject in Lukács, there's a linked universalizing epistemological function implied here for the novel: Lukács straightforwardly argues that the novel reveals for us what modern consciousness is like, qua consciousness, in its individual totality. In fact, this novelistic Hegelian form is what "truth" looks like, the search for truth that is universal human condition of modernity. That sort of universalist epistemology is no longer a very fashionable academic pursuit or admission; far from constituting a new materialist or ecological perspective, the novel as a form reeks of anthropocentric, neo-imperialist, white male privilege in its lauding such a heroic imposing of order on an otherwise "meaningless" world.

But as theoretically unfashionable as this explanation is in the present, it's likewise hard to see where, on the broad outlines, Lukács is "wrong" about this "theory of the novel"—at least where he's wrong about the historical fact that the novel is the quintessential form of European, alienated modernist humanism, and the characteristic Copernican, phenomenological turn of Anthropocene thought: both Kant and the rise of the novel become linked sites where "life" became myopically centered on human subjects and the (endless?) search to project a world that made sense to us, thereby carving out a central place for our Sisyphean task in ordering that meaningless nature. In short, Lukács shows us that the novel is the modern bourgeois form par excellence, and I can't quite see how he's "wrong" about that, historically speaking.

And now that we no longer live so comfortably within the worldview of that anthropomorphic Eurocentric humanism or modernity, this seems to raise again the obvious question: Whither humanism's primary form (the novel) in an age of posthumanism?

A parallel question arises concerning whether contemporary twenty-first century autofiction, which finds itself very suspicious of the universalist mansplaining that Lukács lays out as the novel's primary function, can finally evade this phenomenological problem of novelistic form, or whether contemporary autofiction is forced merely to ignore it by focusing on content (thick description of a particular identity), when no matter what any given novel is about, it is in fact the form of the novel that tethers it to anthropomorphic solipsism? As no less an authority than the *New York Times* sums up the condition of fiction circa 2019,

> Not so long ago, the big, ambitious social novel, the novel that wanted to tell us about "the way we live now" or "the state of the nation"—the novel as exemplified by Don DeLillo's "Underworld" (1997) or Jonathan Franzen's "The Corrections" (2001)—enjoyed a prestige and cultural centrality that, in recent years, have come to seem distinctly suspect. Looking increasingly through the lens of identity, some critics have begun to see the universalizing impulse behind such books—their belief in their ability to write across differences of race and class and gender— as presumptuous if not outright aggressive, a kind of epistemological gate-crashing (especially when the author is a well-off white man). One result of this development is that readers have become skeptical when a novel about, say, a white Midwestern family bills itself, and is celebrated as, a novel about America at large. Another result is a spike in books of radical imaginative humility, in which a first-person narrator—usually a more or less transparent proxy for the author—disavows altogether the power to represent the wider world or inhabit the hearts and minds of others. Instead, these novels, by authors like Sheila Heti and Jenny Offill, center on a richly turbulent subjectivity, a welcome corrective to manly bloat and overreach.[12]

The contemporary movement of the novel, on this rendering, traces a course from what we might call Lukácsean or universalizing fiction (the big, ambitious social novel that wanted to tell everyone about "the way we live now") to a form of contemporary autofiction that consists largely of "books of radical imaginative humility, in which a first-person narrator—usually a more or less transparent proxy for the author—disavows altogether the power to represent the wider world or inhabit the hearts and minds of others."

Whatever one thinks of this contemporary movement from the "manly bloat" of big, omniscient fiction to the "welcome corrective" of autofiction, my primary point here is that such a movement can't escape—in fact it almost perfectly mirrors—the formal movement that Lukács charts from Kant's universalizing ambitions for subjectivity (deploying the a priori categories we all share to make sense of the world in a uniform way) to Hegel's radically individualizing ones. For Hegel, the individual's endless and restless novelistic search for identity or recognition makes up a human life, any and all human life, and that life's search for meaning is the only "truth" of our time: as Hegel memorably puts in the *Phenomenology*, "the True is thus the Bacchanalian revel in which no member is not drunk."[13] Such a movement from universal categories to individual affective experience is in fact the epistemological move that made the novel into the form for "everyone" in the nineteenth century; so it would seem that in the present, we can hardly unproblematically escape such a high-philosophical "universalizing impulse" merely by doubling down on that very same Hegelian maneuver 200 years later. If the age of autofiction is the era of "richly turbulent subjectivity," we would do well to remember that announcement was originally brought to you by the phenomenological turn to subjectivity in late eighteenth-century and early nineteenth-century Europe.

In the end, it remains more or less settled law that the novel is primarily the solution to a modernist phenomenological problem: how to make semicoherent, temporary sense of subjective experience? And the answers offered by Kant, Hegel, and the novel are similar—sense or meaning is produced by a subject's imposing a temporary narrative order (time, space, causality) on that flow of experience or life. The Copernican Revolution of the eighteenth century suggests that meaning, insofar as it's available at all, resides in the subject (its desires and modes of organization—its projection of a meaningful "world"), not in the objects or experiences themselves. And this is a truth that you can learn as easily from Kant's *Prolegomena to Any Future Metaphysics* as you can from Daniel Defoe's *Robinson Crusoe*.

Most critics (and moreso post-critics) today don't want much to do with Kant's or Hegel's universalizing explanations of anything and everything, much less Robinson Crusoe's (remember that he's stranded on the island largely because of his eager participation in the slave trade, not to mention his Euro-anthropocentric claims of imperialist dominion over the island and his scandalous treatment of Friday and other indigenous people of the novel); but if we return to the question of literature's relevance to the post- or inhuman (or to anything else for that matter), I think most critics' responses concerning the importance of the novel almost have to fall back on Hegel and Kant—we recognize in the novel something of the structure of human experience as our common striving for individual identity and meaning, and this is edifying in some way (even if in the novel we recognize the limits of our knowledge, which is surely Kant's major theme as well).

This, for example, is Jacques Derrida's gambit in his final lecture course, *The Beast and the Sovereign 2*, where he compares Defoe's *Robinson Crusoe* to Martin Heidegger's 1929–30 lecture series concerning various life forms' ability (or lack thereof) to engage in the projection of a world. Recall that for Heidegger, the capacity to project a world (*Weltbildung*) is the sole purview of human Dasein, while animals are sadly *weltarm*, poor in world, and the stones of the earth are *weltlos*, worldless or completely unable to project a world of possibility or futurity. Throughout his lectures, Derrida wonders about this Heideggerian truism: Derrida questions whether animals have access to a greater or lesser realm of possibility attached to the idea of "world," certainly, but even moreso whether there is such a thing as "a" shared world for us privileged humans. Maybe, as Derrida argues in thinking Defoe against Heidegger, "there is no world; there are only islands."[14] In any case, the common (but not shared) irreducibility of the individual living thing's encounter with finitude— as Derrida puts it, death for any organism is "each time unique, the end of the world"—remains the epistemological or ontological privilege of the fiction of the world in Derrida, as much as in Heidegger: all living things, to one extent or another, project a world. But if you argue, in posthuman or new materialist sense, that "living," for whatever kind of entity (say, a meadow of switchgrass, polar ice sheets, or the myriad ecosystems of the earth itself) is not equivalent to "projecting a world" of fictional choice or possibilities among which an individuated being or entity must decide, then it seems to me that Derrida— and with him, most of this "life = projecting a world" philosophy—is on this point left without a leg to stand on.[15]

More than that, though, the problem for fiction's potential as an ethical or political driver of anything in particular, much less a savior from our humanist prison house, is that it's a hopelessly individualist form of anthropomorphic enterprise. Grander philosophical questions about world projection aside (as in the Derridean question about whether any given fiction is finally a whole world of shared human sense or only small island of solipsism), when it comes to actually reading a novel, either way it's just me and the book—on the subway, in the break room at work, in the library, or in the easy chair at home. Contemporary autofiction doesn't solve this problem, but in fact intensifies it by ironically distributing it everywhere on the formal level: no one can speak for or about anyone or anything but his, her, or their own individual experience. Other (less popular) literary forms can boast some collectivity that might lead outside the individual subject toward a post- or inhuman collectivity (the illocutionary force on display at a poetry reading, e.g., or the drama performed by the local theater group); but fiction is an utterly individual and individualizing form (which is why, according to Ian Watt's canonical account in *The Rise of the Novel*, the newly minted novel triumphs over other literary forms in the bourgeois European eighteenth century—or one might add, why it remains the dominant literary form in the neoliberal present: the novel's form as well as its content consists of nothing other than the experience of privatized, alienated subjectivity). In short, if a kind of new materialist force, rather than an old-fashioned socially constructed linguistic meaning, enacts the inhuman or posthuman potential of literature (language as unleashing a series of forceful Deleuzean order-words rather than sheltering hidden meanings), then I think we need to see the novel as a residual cultural form going forward.

You can always, as a wide range of theorists from Martha Nussbaum to Dorothy Hale try to do, take this subject-centered necessity of the novel and try to make it into a paradoxical plus, by insisting that it's no longer an old-fashioned liberal humanist subject who reads a novel, in search of certainty or edification, but today's reader constitutes a "new ethical" (Hale's term) decision maker open to change and development: an always-adapting reader who makes the ethical choice not to be shut out from, but in tune with, the shifting circumstances or his, her, or their world. As Hale writes in "Fiction as Restriction: Self-Binding in New Ethical Theories of the Novel,"

> What distinguishes the new ethical account of novel reading from the old ethical account of novel reading is this new conceptualization of the reading subject as engaging in self-restriction as an act of free will. And what distinguishes this new theory of ethical choice from an older theory of the autonomous liberal subject is the self-consciously unverifiable status of the alterity that the ethical subject seeks to produce—an unverifiability that retains the post-structuralist's skepticism about knowledge as a tool of hegemony while bestowing upon epistemological uncertainty a positive ethical content.[16]

Say what you will about this account of the "new" ethics and its "positive" rendering of novelistic uncertainty and subjective decision, but it's awfully hard to distinguish this from the "old" account provided by Lukács or Hegel, neither of whom comes anywhere near suggesting the world (much less the novel!) is a place where anything like objective "verifiability" or edification is on offer.[17] All there is in the novel, for Lukács anyway, is the subject and its experience. Indeed, the defining characteristics of almost all post-Kantian continental thinking—not just post-structuralism—concern a thoroughgoing anti-realist "skepticism about knowledge" coupled with the sense that any otherness a subject might confront isn't actually found in the world, but is rather constituted by an "alterity that the ethical subject seeks to produce" out of its own head.

When Hale summarizes such new attempts to theorize novel reading as ethics itself[18] (in her work as well as the work of Geoffrey Galt Harpham and J. Hillis Miller), I think we can finally see how little daylight there is between the "new" and "old" account of liberal humanist subjectivity:

> In binding herself to the law of novel reading, the reader has thus not simply voluntarily submitted to the alterity of narrative, but actively taken responsibility for the ethical judgments that she projects as the law of novelistic story telling. The reader is for Miller, as much as she is for Harpham, the judge, the executive. And her "leap in the dark" is the experience of vulnerability that new ethicists say comes with decision-making, the necessity of making decisions for oneself that places "I alone" at the center of ethical judgments that cannot be verified by any outside source.[19]

Whether this describes an "old" or "new" understanding of subjectivity, such an entrepreneurial sense of "ethics"—where "I alone," self-declared as "the judge, the executive," remain the undisputed "center of ethical judgments"—seems more in tune with, rather than at variance toward, the every-man-for-himself neoliberal world of constant adaptation and change in which we presently live. And if we have to promote either the supposedly "old" liberal subject (who was at least understood as a little bundle of rights *and social responsibilities*) or what looks like an aggressively neoliberal "new" notion of subjectivity (where "making decisions for one-self [...] cannot be verified by any outside source"), I would opt for the former rather than the latter, precisely because the "liberal" subject's actions refer for verification to an "outside source," not just itself. The old school of obligation to the social world seems much more ethically promising against the day of neoliberalism than this new ethics of radically individual decision-making—or so any American who voted against Donald Trump in 2020 might attest.

Of course, there does exist a kind of meditative function for literary reading or writing that's explicitly designed to dislodge the reader from such a closed, subject–object loop between any individual reading practice and some kind of decisionism concerning the work's upshot or its "meaning": think, for example, of the repetitive, mantra-like wordplay you see in much poetry, especially experimental poetry (figures as disparate as Gertrude Stein and Jack Kerouac), or in fragmented lyric poetry like Claudia Rankine's or Charles Bernstein's. In this context, one could even cite the central canonical poem of the Western twentieth century, T. S. Eliot's "The Waste Land," whose aggressively paratactic structure leads the poem not to any narrative-style conclusion or resolution; rather, it ends on a repetitive mantra: "Shantih shantih shantih." On the flip side of that self-overcoming power of poetic language, however, sits the novel, a form that—in all but its most experimental, nonnarrative instantiations—is not well suited to such a post-, non-, or anti-egoic brand of reading, precisely because the novel as a form is addressed to individual readers who are tasked with making meaning by projecting themselves into the confines of a developing fictional world.

In any case, if in the age of climate disaster we posthuman new materialists no longer so blithely affirm the Kantian or Hegelian story about "reality" (it is what we make it, what we decide it is, because everything pivots on the human subject—nature is essentially meaningless and requires our projection of sense onto or into it), then that would also seem to implicate the novel, the most intense marker for that idea of an inert world awaiting ordering by bourgeois Westerners. If we are striving to move beyond humanism or living through an emergent new materialist realism concerning the vibrancy of all things (as opposed to the drama of modernist humanism, tasked with projecting wonder and a sense of meaning into a lifeless world of mere matter), then what happens to the novel as the official literary form of that bygone, modernist era of the bourgeois subject? My sense is that if we're burying subjectivist European humanism of the Kantian–Hegelian variety, we might as well put the novel in the coffin as well, as they have been coevolved entities, and today neither one is able to live comfortably now that its native habitat has been destroyed.

In the end, this is among the lessons that we can still learn from Lukács today. If nothing else, Lukács is more than willing to harshly criticize his earlier work in light of later developments, most infamously in his 1962 Preface to a reprint of the 1919 book on the novel:

> Thus, if anyone today reads *The Theory of the Novel* in order to become more intimately acquainted with the pre-history of the important ideologies of the 1920s and 1930s, he will derive profit from a critical reading of the book. [...] But if he picks up the book in the hope that it will serve him as a guide, the result will be only a still greater disorientation. (22–23)

Learning from Lukács on this point, I would strongly argue that we needn't abandon the study of the novel—any more than this chapter walks away from the importance of Lukács's *Theory of the Novel*, even though in 1962 he counsels his readers "rightly, to reject it root and branch" (23) as a diagnosis that can survive long after its native historical moment of composition in the midst of the First World War. Following Lukács's clear-eyed caveats about not confusing a history with a guide, perhaps today we should no longer worry so much about the adequacy of this or that diagnosis of the novel, but far rather wonder about whether the novel itself remains a privileged cognitive map for understanding the present or the future of twenty-first century cultural production, given the fact that the novel increasingly seems an anachronistic historical form. And maybe that problematic, to return to where we began this chapter, is among the primary ongoing questions for extinction and/as literature in the present. Perhaps the critical task today is not simply looking at how any given novel represents or comments on questions of extinction, but in addition taking into account the uneasy fact that literary forms may themselves be undergoing a kind of extinction event. As went the epic, so goes the novel?

## Elegy for the Novel

At this point, I have to admit that I seem largely alone in my skepticism concerning the novel as the forceful vanguard of literary production today and going forward: at present, the novel is a completely hegemonic literary form. As an example of such literary dominance, I would note that of the "New York Times 100 Notable Books for 2018," only three of them were poetry volumes—one penned by the year's poet laureate of the United States (Tracy K. Smith), one by the director of the New York Public Library's Schomberg Center for Research in Black Culture (Kevin Young), and one by Homer (*The Odyssey* in a new translation by Emily Wilson). The category of "fiction" (among a series of genres like nonfiction, essays, history, sports, biography, current events, and the like) for the year boasts a collection of 48 notable books—though one of them, oddly enough, is *The Odyssey* in a new translation by Emily Wilson, so we really are down to two poetry volumes for the year. All of this of course suggesting that there's roughly 24 times more notable fiction than poetry being produced today, and that overall only 2 percent of the "notable" books published in 2018 can be classified as con-temporary poetry (and 100 percent of those poetry titles, it turns out, were penned by African Americans). So it seems we live in a golden era for African-American poetry (which I actually think is true); but on the whole, it's fair to surmise that poetry as a cultural form is not seen as much of a significant driver when it comes to assessing the wider, more "notable" literary world. Poetry enjoys polling numbers akin to those tallied for Tulsi Gabbard's Democratic 2020 presidential bid. (Both 2019's and 2020's *New York Times* notable book list each contains 3 percent poetry titles, thereby eclipsing Gabbard's numbers to approach John Hickenlooper's 2020 presidential-primary territory; but all in all things haven't changed much for poetry's popularity in recent years.)

And if fiction, or more narrowly the novel, rules the roost at the popular end of the literary spectrum in places like the *New York Times*, it's worth noting that fiction enjoys similarly hegemonic prestige and saturation within recent academic literary criticism and theory—much of which has come to equate "fiction" or "the novel" with "literature" itself. For example, Amy Hungerford's influential *Making Literature Now* concerns itself exclusively with fiction writers; Mark McGurl's history of creative writing's rise in the university, *The Program Era*, also looks solely at fiction (subtitle: *Postwar Fiction and the Rise of Creative Writing*). As Hale comments on this tendency in her review of scholarship in the ethics of reading, "Over and over again, I discovered that discussions about the ethical value of 'literature' turned out to be discussions about the ethical value of novels."[20] In each of these cases, "literature," "the ethics of reading," or "creative writing" itself each respectively becomes synonymous with "fiction." For my narrowcast purposes here, as I've noted above, fiction is by far the least interesting literary genre, insofar as the novel as a form boasts the least intense or necessary connection with the extralinguistic, post- or inhuman performative forces of new materialism. In contrast to narrative fiction, both drama and poetry have long drunk deeply from the spring of extralinguistic performativity, an immaterial force deployed among the words but not reducible to a conundrum concerning their "meaning."

And while Hungerford would undoubtedly disagree with my dismissive critique of fiction in the present, or might agree but suggest that close reading or individual meaning making does not make a network of fiction producers and consumers, she does decisively suggest that things are changing in the world of writing fiction. She argues, in her lauding of various writing "scenes" (e.g., the McSweeney's crowd in San Francisco), that "making literature now" has moved away from the modernist or postmodernist drama wherein a solitary genius tries to innovate his or her way out of a cloistered drawing room into a cutting-edge global book market—on the figure most intensely of David Foster Wallace, who Hungerford argues we should not read, largely because of his misogyny. Rather, Hungerford suggests that literary production has become a kind of local cottage enterprise, one that tends to be situated in a particular place, scene, and aesthetic.

As she argues concerning Dave Eggers and his involvement with various McSweeney's projects, thinking about any given book's meaning tends to make us "misunderstand the ways that buying books—or more generally, reading—is related to the social scenes from which Eggers's various ventures arise and to which they often seem to return."[21] Though of course some writers (like Eggers) within any particular scene will have a chance of becoming more widely known, much of making literature going forward, Hungerford suggests but doesn't come right out and say, will be somewhat akin to being a popular musician: there's a scene that your band grows out of, a local vibe that conditions your initial sound or style, and at first you have local fans, play local gigs. If you're a local-scene musician, you of course have some chance of going viral (producing a hit song), but the vast majority of solo performers or people in bands will never be able to quit their day jobs and make a living playing music. So, Hungerford suggests between the lines, it will likely go with writing fiction—not a matter of national or international fame and fortune, but a local ethics of care and recognition: "In McSweeney's publications and its reader networks[,] love and friendship is the affective tenor of the interpersonal links that McSweeney's calls into being."[22]

As provocative as Hungerford's analysis proves, in addition to my skepticism about the novel being a producer of much widespread cultural significance going forward, I likewise don't see the novel as a particularly promising niche-market "scene-produced" literary form—insofar as either writing fiction or reading it remains largely a solitary exercise that take place within language and the narrative time of unfolding meaning. The novel has a performative dimension, to be sure, but that dimension takes place largely on the level of a plot's unfolding in language, and within the mechanics of individual readers making meaning. As a form that implies a "way of life," literature as the novel presages life as a lonely road. And while the picture of "novelist as solitary genius" is undoubtedly a holdover that requires demystification, even today we still don't tend to think of the great novelists as having been produced by a school of writing or an artistic scene.

In any case, however narratively driven any given poem or play might be, poetry's and drama's preferred (though by no means exclusive) delivery systems—which is to say, the performed play or the read poem—depend crucially on a kind of performative context and "scene" (the local in-crowd at the bookstore, the theater, the bar) in a way that fiction does not. So it seems odd to suggest that if "scenes" are what "making literature now" is all about, we pay such little attention to poetry or drama. Even long-form narrative television is a collective enterprise—the screen is crowded with actors, the shots composed by armies of technicians, online fan sites allow hardcores to swap theories, and so on. It may well be that fiction writing is becoming more like contemporary poetry or other local, scene-driven artforms in this way, as Hungerford argues; but it seems to me if that's the case, then historically speaking American poetry or drama should be the template discourses for "making literature now," rather than fiction.

In fact, poet David Antin made such a project (quite literally making literature in and of the now, literature as a series of actions rather than as a consumable product) into his life's work: not writing finished poems to be read, but giving improvised "talks" to live, responding audiences—talks that would later be published in lines, as talk-poems. In fact, Antin's itinerary for his poetic project corresponds quite closely to what Hungerford wants to claim for fiction today, the care and maintenance of lively writing scenes rather than a focus on finished works being read by strangers in isolation. For his part, Antin sums up his aesthetics like this: "theres a situation and you respond to it"; "even if i write i dont come to read / i come to talk." As Antin expands on his method for making literature in the now:

                                                              when
    i went somewhere i wanted to make things happen because

    it seemed to me that the art of poetry was the act of making

    poetry not distributing it.[23]

For Antin, poetry is a way of life, not a way of producing artifacts in isolation to be in turn consumed by others in private. Art, of whatever kind, is concerned with responding to the present, and for Antin, that's finally "what it means to be avant-garde" today.

In fact if "scenes" are the new way of making literature now, I would likewise note that twentieth-century American poetry remains to this day routinely understood, written about, and taught as a series of just such local schools or scenes: the Imagist Pound Era (recall that Ezra Pound and William Carlos Williams met as students at the University of Pennsylvania); the Harlem Renaissance north of 125th Street; the Beats (many of whom met below 125th Street, at Columbia University); Confessional Poets in the Robert Lowell Boston lineage (Sylvia Plath and Anne Sexton, most famously); the New York School (part one of Frank O'Hara and John Ashbery, friends since their days at Harvard in the late 1940s, and part two with figures like Ted Berrigan and Bernadette Mayer, the proto-hippie scene surrounding St. Mark's in Greenwich Village); the San Francisco Renaissance of Robert Duncan and Jack Spicer (located in a series of North Beach bars); the Black Mountain writers who clustered around the College; the Black Arts movement; "Language" poetry (centered in New York City and Berkeley, with outposts in Philadelphia and Washington, DC); Nuyorican poetry and the café; the avant-garde scenes surrounding the Brown, Buffalo, and Maine writing programs over the past few decades; Conceptual Writing and Flarf, with their home "scenes" on the internet; and so on. If nothing else, poets like Ashbery and O'Hara are going to the same poetry readings, bars, and art openings in and around New York—in short, they're participating in the same scene, as are many of the Black Arts, San Francisco Renaissance, Language, Beat, or Black Mountain writers. Poets, however begrudgingly, often understand themselves—or at least are understood by critics—in terms of a place or a movement. Fiction writers like DeLillo and Pynchon, not so much.

Now certainly mainstream American poetry of the past 40 years—dominated by the confessional, voice, or "craft" tradition associated with Lowell—makes the privatized subjectivism of today's autofiction look positively humble by comparison: contemporary American poetry of the mainstream "workshop" variety is utterly and completely dominated by the voice of a poetic "I" sharing highly sculpted personal insights about everyday experience. That hegemony led Lyn Hejinian to rebuke in 1989:

> I don't write to discover, define, describe, disclose my Self, whatever that is, nor to share my epiphanous experiences of the small, intimate, everyday moments. To be honest, I'm scornful of writing that aims at anything like that. I think that the popularity, such as it is, of personal poetry is the result of other factors. Epiphanous experience of or within moments of daily American white life, for example, are predictable. The little poems charged by these moments represent that reassuring predictability, that sense of order and virtue, which sustains the illusion of the genuineness of the emotions captured there.[24]

Contemporary mainstream American poetry has, despite Hejinian's critique, continued as a nearly impenetrable safe haven for that privatized neoliberal "I," probably even moreso than the novel; but the point I want to insist on here—and going all the way back through Lukács—is that, *unlike the novel, poetry as a form wasn't always beholden to reporting the privatized experience of an individual, humanist narrative voice; nor was poetry as a form born alongside the bourgeois Western subject as its official expressive vehicle.*

Poetry, and not only the epic poetry that Lukács discusses but myriad other poetic forms, has had any number of other jobs over the past 3000 or so years, since Homer: for millennia, poetry has been performing collective work that has been memorial, historical, ceremonial, competitive, religious, seductive, entertaining, edifying, meditative, time-passing, musical, dramatic (ancient to early modern tragic drama is likewise poetry), as well as serving dozens of other functions. By contrast, that relative newcomer the novel does boast (at least up to this point) a distinguished record of accomplishments on its several-century-long CV; but all through that period of immense productivity the novel has held only one job: tell the story of bourgeois subjective experience. And in the present, it seems to me that primary novelistic task has either (1) been largely taken over by other nonlinguistic forms, most notably long-form narrative streaming video; and/or (2) shown itself to be a kind of rearguard operation in a world looking to escape from myopic individualized anthropomorphism associated with solitary reading and writing, the novel's primary delivery systems.

So the question going forward seems obvious: Can the novel find something else to do, find work other than the narration of an individual subject's experience, however capaciously understood? (E.g., Paul Auster's novel *Timbuktu*, narrated by a dog, shows us that individual experience or narrative voice doesn't have to be human, however cautious we might remain about anthropomorphizing in such an instance; on the other hand, regardless of what the novel is "about," the second half of the novelistic equation, the reading experience, remains ineluctably individual and privatized.) I honestly don't know the answer to this question of what *else* the novel can do, though the novel's much older siblings, poetry and drama, have proven to be quite elastic and adaptable forms over the centuries. But it does return me to wondering over the question of the novel's almost complete hegemony in both popular and critical discourse, and whether there's a kind of radical disconnect between the novel as a form (born as the favorite artistic child of European bourgeois individualism) and the contemporary posthuman or new materialist situation that's desperate to pass beyond that very same bourgeois humanism. Is this predicament the novel's endgame, an elegy for the novel? Or is literature itself, regardless of its forms, doomed going forward in a visual and affective new materialist world, beyond language?

I actually don't think so: in a world where short bursts of "poetic" language on Twitter or Instagram, for better or worse, make decisive differences, and where "dramatic" performativity likewise is decisive in sculpting the human and nonhuman landscapes (witness everything from politicians posturing to ice floes falling into the sea to the status of matter itself), I would maintain that poetry and drama remain decisive, not only for thinking about the world today, but for thinking beyond the human. About the novel, I have my doubts.

# EPILOGUE: WHERE I PREDICTABLY ASSERT THAT THE KIND OF THING I DO IS THE KEY

> Every discipline sustains itself "in theory"—a discipline's coherence derives not from the objects it examines, but rather from the concepts and methods it mobilizes to generate critical thought.
>
> —D. N. Rodowick, *Elegy for Theory*

As we've seen throughout, even the most full-throated defenses of literary study in the present do not foreground the centrality of literature qua literature, because that's actually impossible without first deploying a theory that would locate for you the prized literariness of said texts. Rather, literary study (today, as in the past) foregrounds the primacy and value of certain kinds of theoretical approach. Perhaps the most persuasive theoretical apology for literature in the present puts forward a mode of "literary" attention as deep, hyperaware, hesitant, responsive to possibility—and lauds the concomitant effects that special brand of literary acumen might have in the world (leading to increased human empathy and care, deliberative hesitation rather than haste, an opening toward the anti-capitalist good life, and so forth). As Christopher Schaberg sums it up in *The Work of Literature in an Age of Post-Truth*, a large "part of the work of literature" is that "it slows us down, helps us focus on the things closest to us, if, then, possibly to engage these things more thoughtfully, more respectfully."[1] Fair enough, though one might wonder whether such a justification of careful reading will have strayed very far from Cold War, new critical imperatives—where the reader avoids at all costs laying a preexisting interpretive template over the literary object in order to burnish his, her, or their free and autonomous aesthetic power of judgment.

However, the project of slowing down puts me more immediately in mind of Nietzsche's defense of philology in the introduction to *Daybreak* (published in 1881, though this introduction was itself written very slowly, and attached to the book five years later):

It is not for nothing that I have been a philologist, perhaps I am a philologist still, that is to say, a teacher of slow reading: in the end I also write slowly. Nowadays it is not only my habit, it is also to my taste—a malicious taste, perhaps?—no longer to write anything which does not reduce to despair every sort of man who is "in a hurry." For philology is that venerable art which demands of its votaries one thing above all: to go aside, to take time, to become still, to become slow—it is a goldsmith's art and connoisseurship of the *word* which has nothing but delicate, cautious work to do and achieves nothing if it does not achieve it *lento*. But for precisely this reason it is more necessary than ever today, by precisely this means does it entice and enchant us the most, in the midst of an age of "work," that is to say, of hurry, of indecent and perspiring haste, which wants to "get everything done" at once, including every old or new book: this art does not so easily get anything done, it teaches to read *well*, that is to say, to read slowly, deeply, looking cautiously before and aft, with reservations, with doors left open, with delicate eyes and fingers.... My patient friends, this book desires for itself only perfect readers and philologists.[2] (ellipsis in original)

Whatever else it is, this theory of "slow reading" constitutes an eloquent defense of the values associated with close and sustained attention, and in addition Nietzsche does seem admirably able to encompass aspects of both the "anti-capitalist" (Clune) and the "ethical" (Dettmar and Starr, Hale) agendas for thinking about literature that we discussed in Chapters 1 and 2. But for all its continued salience, let me just note that the 140 years since Nietzsche penned this love letter to his home discipline have not been kind to the academic study of philology, and such a defense of meticulous slowness seems unlikely to fare much better when it comes to defending the discipline of literary study within the corporate university of the twenty-first century, or to hold much sway among the perennially distracted students in our media-saturated landscape. Likewise, it's worth wondering about how or why this Nietzschean nineteenth-century defense of philology—essentially, its primary usefulness is that it has no immediate worldly utility—can so seamlessly be imported as a defense of other humanities disciplines, in a vastly different time, place, and institutional situation.[3]

The "one-size-fits-all" quality of slow reading as a project suggests once again that any value one might attach to this practice rests solely in its theoretical orientation, rather than anything inherent in the historical situation (in either the nineteenth or twenty-first centuries) or anything that's tethered essentially to the disciplinary objects (literature, philology, philosophy, history, and the like). While literature privileges, in Schaberg's words, "being

able to read slowly, to carefully consider how narratives are fabricated, produced, disseminated and consumed,"[4] at the end of the day nothing about
the novel qua novel disables a reader from skimming it—any more than
something inherent in philology disallows hasty translation or sloppy historical reference. On Schaberg's account (and many more like it in the present),
literature "itself" is ironically but inexorably unmoored from any necessary
role in fostering such slow methodological care and attention. And Schaberg
straightforwardly admits as much: "for me, literature has also included
airports, advertisements, long walks, Lego toys, and art, among myriad other
things" (5).

    In short, and in polemical conclusion, the work of literature in the present
has inexorably become the work of theory—learning privileged methodological modes that can resonate productively with all things great and small,
everything from airports to Lego blocks. Which is to say, the work of literature
on this rendering has become the theoretical or methodological attribute of
a certain mode of practice—an orientation or a way of life—not an attribute
inexorably attached to any given disciplinary object or set of objects. As a
mode of theoretical orientation, such critical engagement, which I think
we can no longer simply call "reading" or "interpretation," is equally available and useful for thinking about anything and everything, and is no more
contained "in" a novel than it is "in" an advertisement or a child's toy or the
flora and fauna you'd encounter on a long walk in the woods.

    In the end, the literature department has become, whether most of us like
it or not, primarily a theory department, training students in approaches,
modes, and forms of critical response—whether that consists of close or distant reading, new ethical response, anti-capitalist critique, historicisms old or
new, the empathy of walking a mile in someone else's shoes, historical or postcolonial inquiry, feminism or queer theory, ecocriticism and animal studies,
critical race theory, posthumanism, or any of a hundred other old and new
theoretical provocations. And this is the case at least partially because the
disciplinary objects that are the bread and butter of English and other literature departments—whether in the end that means novels, poems, drama,
films, videos, popular culture, and the like—can't any longer carry centralized
canonical weight: we can't any longer pretend there is "a" history of any given
national literature (or even that the project of studying a national literature
is defensible at all); and we'll likewise have to admit that there is no "great
American novel" on the horizon—a novel that could pretend to speak definitively about "the" experience of being American. And to be frank, we haven't
been able to defend such a cultural "greatness" model of literature for quite
some time, at least since the long-overdue demise of new criticism as the dominant theoretical paradigm.

So let's face reality: literature departments are already a series of theory departments, primarily invested in teaching biopolitical techniques and methodological orientations that could be placed into productive resonance with almost any objects. Even, one might say especially, the few remaining bow-tied old white guys who "believe in literature" and hate newfangled "theory" are nevertheless actually shilling for a biopolitical way of life (nostalgia) and/or a methodological approach (appreciation), not finally defending a series of literary objects.

Mea culpa time: I doubt that the realization "we're all theorists now" is going to bolster us in the downsizing meeting with the provost or bring back majors in droves, but there hopefully is at least a certain kind of useful clarity that comes from such a provocation or orientation. And perhaps most importantly, such an understanding and foregrounding of our primary theoretical work allows us to highlight and insist upon the methodological, political, and ethical stakes of literary study, rather than leaving us in the unconscionable position of affirming (however tacitly or unconsciously) the white supremacy that characterizes an overwhelming majority of the literary texts within the historical Euro-American literary canon—or defending the implied claim that familiarity with such literary works is the backbone of "culture" itself.

A final thought: 20 years ago, in his book *The Future of Theory*, Jean-Michel Rabaté suggested a lifeline or a way forward for theory, which was seemingly running out of steam in the early years of the twenty-first century. Recall that in those days, it still looked like the centrality of literature was an unquestionably solid ground for the discipline going forward (both in terms of student credit hours and disciplinary verve measured by MLA attendance and the like), so Rabaté's way to address that crisis of literary studies, and to rescue the fate of the flagging underdog theory, was to tweak our understanding of the relation between literature and theory—no longer seeing theory as a stand-alone discourse apart from or alongside literature, and thereby parasitic upon it, but far rather recasting theory as a subset of its ostensible bedrock and more enduring object, literature. As Rabaté put it in one of his chapter titles, the way forward to the future looked like "Theory Not *of* Literature But *as* Literature."[5] Here, two decades later and with the seemingly unshakeable ground of literature having suffered a number of near-fatal hemorrhages due to the changing mediascape and the temblors of 2008 and 2020, I'm suggesting exactly the opposite for the future of literary studies: Not Theory *of* Literature, but Literature *as* Theory. Not literary studies as putting on offer familiarity with a series of privileged literary texts and their prized cultural "meaning," nor transmuting theory into one of those canonical texts, but literary studies as kind of theoretical orientation, a series of modes of response or ways of doing things.

Most of my colleagues today think about literature like proto-environmentalists used to think about the earth—it would last forever, unless it was destroyed by external means like nuclear war; and thereby environmentalists primarily needed to teach people how to "love" and appreciate the earth. However, just as environmental discourse gets intensified once it accepts that its object—the earth—is in serious trouble, so too I think that literary studies has to confront head-on the sense that its primary object, this baggy thing we call literature, is under threat of extinction. The external "nuclear" threats for literary studies today are easy enough to recognize—the pressure from above exerted by downsizing administrators and neoliberal apologists who see literary study as frivolous at best, dangerous to the university's new vocational mission at worst. And we certainly need to keep those wolves at bay. But I think we also need to confront the pressure from below, so to speak—the fact that the very ground that we think we're standing on requires theoretical shoring up in the present. The academic study of literature requires an elegy because its object doesn't unproblematically exist anymore: which is to say, we have to come to terms with the fact that there is not (and never has been) a way to locate what literature is, or what it can do, without the preexisting condition of a theoretical orientation. Literature as an autonomous object of inquiry is dead. Long live theory.

# NOTES

## 1. Endgames

1 https://connect.chronicle.com/rs/931-EKA-218/images/ChronicleReview_Endg ame.pdf (accessed January 5, 2020); page numbers hereafter cited in the text.

2 One hesitates to cite such stuff in polite scholarly company, but here is Whitman quoted by Horace Traubel: "The nigger, like the Injun, will be eliminated: it is the law of races, history, what-not: always so far inexorable—always to be" (*With Walt Whitman in Camden,* Volume 2, 283: https://whitmanarchive.org/criticism/disciples/traubel/ WWWiC/2/whole.html). The phrase "superber race" is from "the Song of the Red-Wood Tree" (https://whitmanarchive.org/published/LG/1891/poems/93) where to be fair, it refers to ancient trees yielding (or maybe not) to humans rather than any one "race" of humans yielding to another; but in any case it is an apt indication of Whitman's quite literal and hierarchical brand of race-thinking. For example, when asked by Traubel about the fact that his work wasn't exactly popular among the myriad folks he championed in his poems, Whitman reacted: "But it is about as if we said—this sculptor or painter has made us a counterpart of so and so—a nigger, maybe, or an Injun—and there's not a nigger or Injun in America that can appreciate it. But what of *that*? How does *that* settle the question?" (*With Walt Whitman in Camden*, Volume 7, 87: https://whitmanarchive.org/criticism/disciples/traubel/WWWiC/7/whole.html). For more on this issue, see George Hutchinson and David Drews, "Racial Attitudes," in the Walt Whitman Archive: https://whitmanarchive.org/criticism/current/encyc lopedia/entry_44.html (all links last accessed on March 20, 2020).

3 https://english.uchicago.edu/ (accessed June 21, 2020).

4 Ngugi wa Thiong'o, "On the Abolition of the English Department." *Homecoming: Essays* (London: Heinemann, 1972).

5 Geoffrey Chaucer, "General Prologue" to *The Canterbury Tales*, line 10: https://www. poetryfoundation.org/poems/43926/the-canterbury-tales-general-prologue (accessed February 12, 2021).

6 The closing refrain from the Sex Pistols' "God Save the Queen." *Never Mind the Bullocks, Here's the Sex Pistols* (London: Virgin Records, 1977).

7 Obama in 2014: "I promise you, folks can make a lot more, potentially, with skilled manufacturing or the trades than they might with an art history degree." https://www. insidehighered.com/news/2014/01/31/obama-becomes-latest-politician-criticize-liberal-arts-discipline (accessed July 2, 2020). The humanities or arts major working as a Starbucks barista, living in the parents' basement, has in fact become a staple of the American higher-education imaginary.

8   Quoted in Elspeth Reeve, "Mitt Romney is America's Most Successful English Major," *The Atlantic* (April 27, 2012). Edited for clarity. https://www.theatlantic.com/politics/archive/2012/04/mitt-romney-americas-most-successful-english-major/328794/ (accessed July 14, 2020).

9   See, e.g., Walter Benn Michaels, *The Trouble with Diversity: How We Learned to Love Identity and Ignore Inequality* (New York: Macmillan, 2006).

10  See Walter Benn Michaels and Adolph Reed, "The Trouble with Disparity," *Common Dreams* (August 15, 2020): https://www.commondreams.org/views/2020/08/15/trouble-disparity (accessed August 11, 2020), where they argue that "racism is real and anti-racism is both admirable and necessary, but extant racism isn't what principally produces our inequality and anti-racism won't eliminate it. And because racism is not the principal source of inequality today, anti-racism functions more as a misdirection that justifies inequality than a strategy for eliminating it."

11  Michael W. Clune, "Judgment and Equality." *Critical Inquiry* 45 (Summer 2019): 910–34, 933.

12  See Thomas Piketty's mammoth and definitive *Capital in the Twenty-First Century*, translated by Arthur Goldhammer (Cambridge, MA: Harvard University Press, 2013).

13  Clune, "Judgment and Equality," 933.

14  Wendell Harris, *Literary Meaning: Reclaiming the Study of Literature* (New York: NYU Press, 1996). This specific wording is taken from the author's summary offered here: https://nyupress.org/9780814735251/literary-meaning/ (accessed September 13, 2020).

15  Michel Foucault, "What Is an Author?" In *The Norton Anthology of Theory and Criticism*, edited by Vincent Leitch, William E. Cain, Laurie A. Fink, Barbara E. Johnson, John McGowan, T. Denean Sharpley-Whiting, and Jeffrey Williams (New York: Norton, 2010, 1475–89), 1483.

16  Michael Bérubé, "Extinction Event." Special issue *The Future of the Academic Work Force, Chronicle of Higher Education* (August 20, 2020): https://www.chronicle.com/article/the-future-of-the-academic-work-force (accessed August 30, 2020).

17  Michel Foucault, *The Order of Things: An Archaeology of the Human Sciences* (New York: Vintage, 1994), 386.

18  Geoffrey Galt Harpham, *The Humanities and the Dream of America* (Chicago: University of Chicago Press, 2011), 15.

19  Geoffrey Galt Harpham, *What Do You Think, Mr. Ramirez? The American Revolution in Education* (Chicago: University of Chicago Press, 2017), xiv.

20  Available here: https://www.vqronline.org/essay/criticism-inc-0 (accessed October 31, 2020).

21  *General Education in a Free Society: Report of the Harvard Committee* (Cambridge: Harvard University Press, 1945), 110: https://archive.org/details/generaleducation032440mbp/page/n133/mode/2up (accessed April 2, 2020).

22  Ibid., 112.

23  Sean Shesgreen, "Canonizing the Canonizer: A Short History of *The Norton Anthology of English Literature*." *Critical Inquiry* 35.1 (2009): 293–318, 318.

24  Ibid., n. 296.

25  Galen Tihanov, *The Birth and Death of Literary Theory* (Stanford: Stanford University Press, 2019). Pages numbers hereafter cited in the text.

26  David Antin, *What It Means to Be Avant-Garde* (New York: New Directions, 1993), 44.

27 Mary Oliver, from "Sometimes." https://static1.squarespace.com/static/58082f96e
6f2e1a9caea07b8/t/5c77665b7817f7033b5a205c/1551328860278/Mary+Oliver+
Poems+in+the+Companion.pdf (accessed May 21, 2020).

## 2. The Novel and New Materialism; or, Learning from Lukács

1 Thomas Pynchon, *The Crying of Lot 49* (New York: Harper and Row, 1986, 82; italics
in original).

2 Diana Coole and Samantha Frost, "Introducing the New Materialisms," in *New
Materialisms: Ontology, Agency and Politics* (Durham, NC: Duke University Press, 2010), 9.

3 Pynchon, *Crying of Lot 49*, 181–82.

4 Ibid., 183.

5 Jane Bennett, "Systems and Things: On Vital Materialism and Object-Oriented
Philosophy." *The Nonhuman Turn*, edited by Richard Grusin (Minneapolis: University
of Minnesota Press, 2015, 223–41), 227.

6 See Margaret Anne Doody, *The Secret History of the Novel* (New Brunswick, NJ: Rutgers
University Press, 1996), which argues straightforwardly that "the Novel as a form of
literature in the West has a continuous history of about two thousand years" (1).

7 Georg Lukács, *The Theory of the Novel*, translated by Anna Bostock (Cambridge,
MA: MIT Press, 1971), 17. Page numbers subsequently given in the text.

8 Friedrich Nietzsche, *The Birth of Tragedy* and *The Case of Wagner*, translated by Walter
Kaufmann (New York: Vintage, 1967), 72.

9 Franco Moretti, "Lukács's *Theory of the Novel*: Centenary Reflections." *New Left Review*
9 (2014): 39–42, 42.

10 For a pointed critique of Lukács's *Theory of the Novel* on this distinction, specifically one
arguing that the novel as a form has its own style of "epic" ambition, albeit an individualist one, see Massimo Fussillo's "Epic, Novel," translated by Michael F. Moore, in *The
Novel, Volume 2: Forms and Themes*, edited by Franco Moretti (Princeton, NJ: Princeton
University Press, 2006), 32–63.

11 Michel Foucault, *Discipline and Punish*, translated by Alan Sheridan (New York: Vintage,
1977), 193.

12 Giles Harvey, "To Decode White Male Rage, He First Had to Write in His Mother's
Voice: How Ben Lerner Reinvented the Social Novel for a Hyper-Self-Obsessed Age."
*New York Times Magazine* (October 8, 2019): https://www.nytimes.com/interactive/
2019/10/08/magazine/ben-lerner-topeka-school.html.

13 G. W. F. Hegel, *Phenomenology of Spirit*, translated by A. V. Miller (Oxford, UK: Oxford
University Press, 1977), 27.

14 Jacques Derrida, *The Beast and the Sovereign, Volume 2*, translated by Geoffrey Bennington
(Chicago: University of Chicago Press, 2011), 9.

15 For an extended rehearsal of this argument, see chapters 2 and 3 of my *Plant
Theory: Biopower and Vegetable Life* (Stanford, CA: Stanford University Press, 2016).

16 Dorothy J. Hale, "Fiction as Restriction: Self-Binding in New Ethical Theories of the
Novel." *Narrative* 15.2 (2007): 187–206, 190.

17 See e.g., Hegel in the *Phenomenology*: "Disparity […] is itself directly present in the True
as such. […] Dogmatism […] is nothing else but the opinion that the True exists in
a proposition which is fixed as a result" (23). As he goes on to insist, and this is 1807,
recall,

> it should be noted that current opinion has already come to view the sci-
> entific regime bequeathed by mathematics as quite old-fashioned—with
> its explanations, divisions, axioms, sets of theorems, its proofs, principles,
> deductions, and conclusions from them. Even if its unfitness is not clearly
> understood, little or no use is any longer made of it; and though not condemned
> outright, no one likes it very much. (28)

18    The "new ethical" claims endorsed by Hale in "Fiction as Restriction" are ironically
       not very restricted:

> The novel reader's experience of free submission, her response to the "hailing"
> performed by the novel, becomes, for these theorists, a necessary condition for
> the social achievement of diversity, a training in the honoring of Otherness,
> which is the defining ethical property of the novel—and is also what makes lit-
> erary study, and novel reading in particular, a crucial pre-condition for positive
> social change. (189)

       While I like literature as much as the next person, I'm not sure how or why anyone
       can so unproblematically classify solitary literary reading as "training in the honoring
       of Otherness," much less suggesting that the simple act of reading novels is "a crucial
       pre-condition for positive [!] social change," or more astonishingly that such reading
       is a "necessary [!] condition for the social achievement of diversity." This constitutes
       humanities magical thinking at its most unrestricted—the idea that the social and pol-
       itical world is finally driven by (the most highly refined?) individuals and their interior
       thoughts. In any case, the "new ethical" prescription seems clear: further complexify
       your bourgeois interiority and that'll change the social world!

19    Ibid., 195.
20    Ibid., 189.
21    Amy Hungerford, *Making Literature Now* (Stanford, CA: Stanford University Press,
       2016), 430.
22    Ibid., 47.
23    David Antin, *Tuning* (New York: New Directions, 1984), 109, 147, 151.
24    Lyn Hejinian and Tyrus Miller, "An Exchange of Letters." *Paper Air* 4.2 (1989): 33–
       40, 35.

## Epilogue: Where I Predictably Assert That the Kind of Thing I Do Is the Key

1    Christopher Schaberg, *The Work of Literature in an Age of Post-Truth* (New York: Bloomsbury
      Academic, 2018), 7.
2    Friedrich Nietzsche, *Daybreak: Thoughts on the Prejudices of Morality*, translated by R. J.
      Hollingdale (Cambridge, UK: Cambridge University Press, 1997), 5.
3    Perhaps the most high-profile version of this argument is Martha Nussbaum's *Not for
      Profit: Why Democracy Needs the Humanities* (Princeton: Princeton University Press, 2017),
      where she defends those narrative values traditionally "associated with the humanities
      and the arts: the ability to think critically; the ability to transcend local loyalties and to
      approach world problems as a 'citizen of the world'; and, finally, the ability to imagine
      sympathetically the predicament of another person" (7).
4    Schaberg, *The Work of Literature*, 143.
5    Jean-Michel Rabaté, *The Future of Theory* (London: Wiley-Blackwell, 2002), 117.

# INDEX OF NAMES